Cooking Light

REGIONAL FARE
COOKBOOK

Cooking Light®

REGIONAL FARE
COOKBOOK

COMPILED AND EDITED BY
SUSAN M. MCINTOSH, M.S., R.D.

Oxmoor
House®

ISBN: 0-8487-2742-8
Printed in the United States of America
First Printing 2002

Previously published as *Low-Fat Ways to Cook Regional Fare*
© 1997 by Oxmoor House, Inc.

Editor-in-Chief: Nancy Fitzpatrick Wyatt
Editorial Director, Special Interest Publications: Ann H. Harvey
Senior Foods Editor: Katherine M. Eakin
Senior Editor, Editorial Services: Olivia Kindig Wells
Art Director: James Boone

Cooking Light® Regional Fare Cookbook

Menu and Recipe Consultant: Susan McEwen McIntosh, M.S., R.D.
Assistant Editor: Kelly Hooper Troiano
Associate Foods Editor: Anne Chappell Cain, M.S., M.P.H., R.D.
Copy Editor: Shari K. Wimberly
Editorial Assistant: Kaye Howard Smith
Indexer: Mary Ann Laurens
Associate Art Director: Cynthia R. Cooper
Designer: Carol Damsky
Senior Photographer: Jim Bathie
Photographers: Howard L. Puckett, Ralph Anderson
Senior Photo Stylist: Kay E. Clarke
Photo Stylists: Cindy Manning Barr, Virginia R. Cravens
Production and Distribution Director: Phillip Lee
Associate Production Manager: Vanessa Cobbs Richardson

Cover: *Chicken-Rice Burritos (recipe on page 43)*
Frontispiece: *Tiramisù (recipe on page 139)*

To order additional publications, call 1-800-633-4910.

**For more books to enrich your life, visit
oxmoorhouse.com**

CONTENTS

REGIONAL DISHES GO LIGHT

From the coast of California to the rocky shores of Maine, this country
is a melting pot of cuisines. Immigrants to the United States have brought with
them a bit of their homelands in the form of family recipes. Although these provided
a rich diversity of foods, many were not always healthy. Now, thanks to a wide
variety of low-fat ingredients and revised cooking methods, you can enjoy ethnic
foods of all types without abandoning your goal to eat less fat.

The Italian homemaker of the past knew nothing about the fat grams in her family's favorite manicotti. Her goal was simply to prepare wholesome meals that all of them would like.

Today, we realize the importance of eating less fat. Read on to see how we've reduced the fat in Four-Cheese Manicotti and over 150 other regional dishes, including French, Greek, Mexican, and Oriental. After you see how it's done, you can cut the fat in your family's favorites, too.

Keep the fat low in Four-Cheese Manicotti (page 103) by using reduced-fat and nonfat cheeses.

MARKET SELECTIONS

The first step to trimming fat from traditional recipes is to start with low-fat ingredients. The following information will help you make nutritious, low-fat choices.

• **Breads, grains, rice, and pasta.** Many varieties of ethnic breads are low in fat. French and Italian bread, bagels, English muffins, pita bread, and tortillas made without oil are all good choices.

Regional dishes are often made with low-fat grains and grain products such as rice, barley, buckwheat, bulgur, oats, and pasta. Just limit any added butter, cheese, cream, and oil.

• **Legumes.** Cuban Black Beans, Cajun Beans and Rice, and Mediterranean Bean Dip are just three examples in this book of regional dishes based on legumes. Beans and other legumes are fat-free and rich in carbohydrate, protein, and fiber.

• **Fruits and vegetables.** Good cooks around the world use an abundance of fruits and vegetables. That's good news since fruits and vegetables are so high in vitamins, fiber, and complex carbohydrates, yet generally low in fat.

Serve Raspberry-Champagne Sorbet (page 130), a French specialty, instead of ice cream to limit the fat in your diet.

If you are purchasing frozen vegetables, choose plain vegetables that have no added fat. Read labels of boil-in-bag products, international style vegetables, and vegetable medleys to choose those that are low in fat.

• **Dairy products.** When it comes to milk, skim is the best choice for low-fat cooking and eating. Two percent milk is not a good low-fat choice because it has about 35 percent of calories from fat.

Substitute plain nonfat yogurt for mayonnaise in many recipes. Low-fat or nonfat sour cream can be used in place of regular sour cream. When buying cheese, choose nonfat or reduced-fat versions that contain 5 grams or less fat per ounce.

• **Meats, poultry, and fish.** Popular in many cuisines, meat and poultry provide valuable protein but also significant amounts of fat. Select only lean cuts of beef, pork, and lamb, and remove skin from poultry before or after cooking. Fish and shellfish are generally low in fat but high in protein. Keep the fat low by using low-fat cooking methods.

For sandwiches, choose lean deli-sliced ham or turkey or turkey-based cold cuts. Avoid regular bologna, salami, and other high-fat lunch meats.

• **Fats and oils.** Whether it's olive oil in Greek dishes or pure butter in French, fat contributes a desirable flavor. However, fat must be limited if you want to follow a healthy diet.

Among fats used in cooking, some are better choices than others. Butter, regular margarine, shortening, and vegetable oils are all 100 percent fat but have varying amounts of saturated, polyunsaturated, and monounsaturated fatty acids. Choose fats and oils that contain the least amount of saturated fat per serving.

Reduced-calorie margarines and spreads can sometimes replace regular butter or margarine but are not recommended for baked products, such as cookies and cakes.

Use vegetable cooking spray to coat skillets, woks, and saucepans for stir-frying and sautéing.

Cut the fat in Oriental Broccoli (page 114) by stir-frying in a nonstick wok coated with cooking spray.

COOKING METHODS

Not only do regional dishes often feature low-fat ingredients but also light cooking methods. For example, many Southwestern dishes call for grilling while the English method is to roast meats. And stir-fries have long been a staple on the Oriental dinner table. Try these and other methods described below to ensure authentic flavor while lowering fat.

• Broil or grill meat, poultry, and fish so that excess fat drips away during cooking.

• Roast meat and poultry on the rack of a roasting pan to allow fat to drip away.

• Stir-fry or sauté meat, poultry, and shellfish in a nonstick skillet coated with vegetable cooking spray.

• Poach fish and poultry in a seasoned fat-free liquid such as water or wine.

• Steam vegetables and fruit in a steamer basket over boiling water.

SEASONING SECRETS

An easy way to get to know a culture's cuisine is to become familiar with its seasonings. Cooks in different cultures tend to rely on many of the same herbs, spices, and natural ingredients. Oregano, for instance, is common to both Mexican and Italian dishes. But because it is combined with different herbs for each cuisine, you get a totally different flavor profile in each.

- *Caribbean:* Allspice, cinnamon, cloves, coriander, curry, garlic, gingerroot, lime, nutmeg, onion, oregano, red pepper, Scotch bonnet peppers and hot sauce, thyme
- *Chinese:* Anise seeds, bean paste, chile oil, garlic, gingerroot, green onions, hot red peppers, sesame oil, sesame seeds, soy sauce, star anise
- *French:* Bay leaves, black pepper, chervil, chives, fines herbes, garlic, green and pink peppercorns, marjoram, nutmeg, onion, parsley, rosemary, shallots, tarragon, thyme
- *German:* Allspice, caraway seeds, cinnamon, dill seeds, dillweed, dry mustard, ginger, mustard seeds, nutmeg, onion, paprika, white pepper
- *Greek:* Cinnamon, dillweed, garlic, lemon, mint, nutmeg, olives, oregano

- *Indian:* Anise seeds, black pepper, cardamom seeds, chiles, cilantro, cinnamon, cloves, coriander seeds, cumin seeds, curry powder, fenugreek (an aromatic Eurasian plant used in curry powder and other spice blends), garlic, gingerroot, mace, mint, mustard seeds, nutmeg, red pepper, saffron, sesame seeds, turmeric, yogurt
- *Italian:* Anchovies, basil, bay leaves, fennel seeds, garlic, marjoram, onion, oregano, parsley, pine nuts, red pepper, rosemary
- *Mexican:* Chiles, cilantro, cinnamon, cocoa, coriander seeds, cumin seeds, garlic, green peppers, lime, onion, oregano, vanilla
- *Spanish:* Almonds, black pepper, cumin seeds, garlic, green peppers, olives, onion, paprika, parsley, saffron

Chinese: sesame seeds, hot red peppers, star anise

French: bay leaves, shallots, green, pink, and black peppercorns

Italian: onion, pine nuts, fennel seeds, garlic, basil, dried oregano

Mexican: cilantro, chiles, cinnamon, lime, garlic

Low-Fat Basics

*W*hether you are trying to lose or maintain weight, low-fat eating makes good sense. Research studies show that decreasing your fat intake reduces risks of heart disease, diabetes, and some types of cancer. The goal recommended by major health groups is an intake of 30 percent or less of total daily calories.

The *Cooking Light Regional Fare Cookbook* helps you meet that goal. It gives you practical, delicious recipes with realistic advice about low-fat cooking and eating. The recipes are lower in total fat than traditional recipes, and most provide less than 30 percent of calories from fat and less than 10 percent from saturated fat.

If you have one high-fat item during a meal, you can balance it with low-fat choices for the rest of the day and still remain within the recommended percentage. For example, fat contributes 48 percent of the calories in the salad for the French menu beginning on page 25. However, because the salad is combined with other low-fat foods, the total menu provides only 16 percent of calories as fat.

The goal of fat reduction is not to eliminate fat entirely. In fact, a small amount of fat is needed to transport fat-soluble vitamins and maintain other normal body functions.

Figuring the Fat

The easiest way to achieve a diet with 30 percent or fewer of total calories from fat is to establish a daily "fat budget" based on the total number of calories you need each day. To estimate your daily calorie requirements, multiply your current weight by 15. Remember that this is only a rough guide because calorie requirements vary according to age, body size, and level of activity. To gain or lose 1 pound a week, add or subtract 500 calories a day. (A diet of fewer than 1,200 calories a day is not recommended unless medically supervised.)

Once you determine your calorie requirement, it's easy to figure the number of fat grams you should consume each day. These should equal or be lower than the number of fat grams indicated on the Daily Fat Limits chart.

Daily Fat Limits		
Calories Per Day	30 Percent of Calories	Grams of Fat
1,200	360	40
1,500	450	50
1,800	540	60
2,000	600	67
2,200	660	73
2,500	750	83
2,800	840	93

Nutritional Analysis

Each recipe in *Cooking Light Regional Fare Cookbook* has been kitchen-tested by a staff of qualified home economists. In addition, registered dietitians have determined the nutrient information, using a computer system that analyzes every ingredient. These efforts ensure the success of each recipe and will help you fit these recipes into your own meal planning.

The nutrient grid that follows each recipe provides calories per serving and the percentage of calories from fat. In addition, the grid lists the grams of total fat, saturated fat, protein, and carbohydrate, and the milligrams of cholesterol and sodium per serving. The nutrient values are as accurate as possible and are based on these assumptions.

• When the recipe calls for cooked pasta, rice, or noodles, we base the analysis on cooking without additional salt or fat.

• The calculations indicate that meat and poultry are trimmed of fat and skin before cooking.

• Only the amount of marinade absorbed by the food is calculated.

• Garnishes and other optional ingredients are not calculated.

• Some of the alcohol calories evaporate during heating, and only those remaining are calculated.

• When a range is given for an ingredient (3 to 3½ cups, for instance), we calculate the lesser amount.

• Fruits and vegetables listed in the ingredients are not peeled unless specified.

Fresh Squeezed Lemonade, Southern Oven-Fried Chicken, Easy Succotash, and Whole-Kernel Corn Bread (menu on page 14)

SENSIBLE DINNERS

*Y*ou don't have to travel across the ocean or even across town to an expensive restaurant to enjoy classic French cuisine. That goes for Tex-Mex, Japanese, and down-home Southern cooking as well. The following pages feature five complete low-fat menus, each typical of a particular region or country.

Use these combinations to guide you as you create your own meal plans from recipes in other chapters of this book. For example, serve Chili Vegetable Tostadas (page 48) along with the salad and coffee featured in the Mexican menu on pages 12 and 13. Another time, try Turkey Enchiladas (page 46).

For an especially fun evening, treat your family or friends to a meal of Alaskan favorites. You'll find a flavorful salmon recipe as well as suggestions on page 17 about how to carry out the Alaskan party theme.

Mexican Beef Salad

MEXICAN SALAD SUPPER

Enjoy this festive Mexican menu that you can prepare for company or family without much effort. Or you may want to serve the beef salad alone as a meal in itself.

Cupping the salad in tortilla bowls adds to the south-of-the-border flair, but the bowls are optional. You may prefer to serve the salad along with crisp-baked tortilla chips. Just cut each tortilla into 6 wedges, place on an ungreased baking sheet, and coat with cooking spray. Then bake at 350° for 8 to 10 minutes or until chips are crisp.

Mexican Beef Salad

Citrus-Jicama Salad

Chilled Mexican Coffee

Serves 6
TOTAL CALORIES PER SERVING: 534
(CALORIES FROM FAT: 23%)

MEXICAN BEEF SALAD

1 pound lean boneless top round steak
1 tablespoon chili powder
½ teaspoon onion powder
½ teaspoon ground oregano
½ teaspoon ground cumin
¼ teaspoon garlic powder
¼ teaspoon ground red pepper
2 teaspoons vegetable oil
1 (8-ounce) carton low-fat sour cream
2 tablespoons canned chopped green chiles
1 teaspoon chili powder
¼ teaspoon ground cumin
⅛ teaspoon garlic powder
6 (10-inch) flour tortillas
Vegetable cooking spray
6 cups shredded iceberg lettuce
1 cup fresh cilantro sprigs
1 cup chopped tomato
¾ cup canned dark red kidney beans, drained
¾ cup frozen whole-kernel corn, thawed
Fresh cilantro sprigs (optional)
Jalapeño pepper slices (optional)

Trim fat from steak. Combine 1 tablespoon chili powder and next 6 ingredients; rub evenly over both sides of steak. Cover and chill 30 minutes.

Combine sour cream and next 4 ingredients in a small bowl. Cover and chill.

Press 1 tortilla into a medium bowl. Microwave at HIGH 1½ minutes or until crisp. Repeat procedure.

Place steak on rack of a broiler pan coated with cooking spray. Broil 5½ inches from heat (with electric oven door partially opened) 5 minutes on each side or to desired degree of doneness.

Cut steak in half lengthwise. Slice each piece of steak diagonally across grain into thin strips.

Combine lettuce and 1 cup cilantro; place lettuce mixture evenly into tortilla bowls. Arrange tomato, beans, corn, and steak over lettuce mixture in each bowl. Spoon sour cream mixture evenly over each serving. If desired, garnish with cilantro sprigs and jalapeño slices. Yield: 6 servings.

PER SERVING: 375 CALORIES (32% FROM FAT)
FAT 13.4G (SATURATED FAT 4.9G)
PROTEIN 26.5G CARBOHYDRATE 37.6G
CHOLESTEROL 62MG SODIUM 341MG

CITRUS-JICAMA SALAD

5 large oranges, peeled and cut crosswise into
    ¼-inch-thick slices
⅔ cup peeled, diced jicama
¼ cup sliced green onions
½ cup unsweetened orange juice
2 tablespoons chopped fresh cilantro
2 tablespoons lime juice
½ teaspoon sugar
⅛ teaspoon ground red pepper

Combine first 3 ingredients. Combine orange juice and remaining 4 ingredients; pour over orange mixture, and toss gently. Cover and chill at least 30 minutes. Serve with a slotted spoon. Yield: 6 (¾-cup) servings.

PER SERVING: 78 CALORIES (2% FROM FAT)
FAT 0.2G (SATURATED FAT 0.0G)
PROTEIN 1.6G CARBOHYDRATE 19.2G
CHOLESTEROL 0MG SODIUM 2MG

CHILLED MEXICAN COFFEE

4¼ cups brewed coffee, chilled
¼ cup chocolate syrup
½ teaspoon ground cinnamon
1½ cups fat-free vanilla ice cream

Combine first 3 ingredients. Pour into individual mugs. Top each serving with ¼ cup ice cream. Serve immediately. Yield: 6 (¾-cup) servings.

PER SERVING: 81 CALORIES (2% FROM FAT)
FAT 0.2G (SATURATED FAT 0.0G)
PROTEIN 2.6G CARBOHYDRATE 17.7G
CHOLESTEROL 0MG SODIUM 49MG

DOWN SOUTH SUNDAY DINNER
(pictured on page 10)

A table loaded with good food and served with a generous portion of hospitality translates to Sunday dinner in the South. It doesn't get much better than that! And when the meal provides only 18 percent of its calories from fat, you've got the best of everything. This is a hearty menu, complete with oven-fried chicken, succotash, and a true Southern favorite, Strawberry Shortcake. Indulge!

Fresh Squeezed Lemonade

Southern Oven-Fried Chicken

Easy Succotash

Whole-Kernel Corn Bread

Strawberry Shortcake

Serves 8
CALORIES PER SERVING: 804
(CALORIES FROM FAT: 18%)

FRESH SQUEEZED LEMONADE

4½ cups water
¾ cup sugar
1¼ cups fresh lemon juice, chilled (about 8 lemons)
Lemon slices (optional)

Combine water and sugar in a medium saucepan; place over high heat, and cook, stirring constantly, until sugar dissolves. Remove from heat; let cool. Pour sugar mixture into a pitcher; chill. Add lemon juice to sugar mixture; stir well. Serve over ice, and garnish with lemon slices, if desired. Yield: 8 (¾-cup) servings.

PER SERVING: 82 CALORIES (0% FROM FAT)
FAT 0.0G (SATURATED FAT 0.0G)
PROTEIN 0.2G   CARBOHYDRATE 22.1G
CHOLESTEROL 0MG   SODIUM 1MG

SOUTHERN OVEN-FRIED CHICKEN

6½ (1-ounce) slices white bread, cubed
⅓ cup all-purpose flour
1 teaspoon salt
1 teaspoon pepper
4 chicken breast halves (about 1½ pounds), skinned
4 chicken thighs (about 1½ pounds), skinned
⅔ cup nonfat buttermilk
Vegetable cooking spray
Assorted fresh vegetables (optional)

Position knife blade in food processor bowl; add bread cubes. Process 30 seconds. Sprinkle crumbs on an ungreased 15- x 10- x 1-inch jellyroll pan. Bake at 400° for 8 minutes or until lightly browned, stirring occasionally. Combine breadcrumbs, flour, salt, and pepper in a large heavy-duty, zip-top plastic bag; set aside.

Combine chicken pieces and buttermilk in another large heavy-duty, zip-top plastic bag. Seal bag, and shake to coat chicken with buttermilk.

Place chicken, 2 pieces at a time, in breadcrumb mixture; seal bag, and shake to coat. Place chicken on a 15- x 10- x 1-inch jellyroll pan coated with cooking spray.

Lightly coat chicken with cooking spray; bake at 400° for 25 minutes. Carefully turn chicken; coat with cooking spray. Bake 25 additional minutes or until done. Garnish individual plates with fresh vegetables, if desired. Yield: 8 servings.

PER SERVING: 220 CALORIES (16% FROM FAT)
FAT 3.9G (SATURATED FAT 1.0G)
PROTEIN 27.6G   CARBOHYDRATE 16.8G
CHOLESTEROL 81MG   SODIUM 519MG

EASY SUCCOTASH

Vegetable cooking spray
¾ cup chopped onion
⅓ cup chopped green pepper
¼ cup chopped reduced-fat, low-salt ham
2 cups frozen lima beans, thawed
2 cups fresh corn cut from cob or frozen corn, thawed
¾ cup water
¼ teaspoon salt
¼ teaspoon pepper
1 cup peeled, chopped tomato

Coat a nonstick skillet with cooking spray; place over medium-high heat until hot. Add onion, green pepper, and ham; sauté until vegetables are tender. Add beans and next 4 ingredients; bring to a boil. Cover, reduce heat, and simmer 20 minutes. Add tomato; stir well. Yield: 8 (½-cup) servings.

PER SERVING: 103 CALORIES (10% FROM FAT)
FAT 1.2G (SATURATED FAT 0.3G)
PROTEIN 5.9G   CARBOHYDRATE 19.3G
CHOLESTEROL 4MG   SODIUM 146MG

WHOLE-KERNEL CORN BREAD

3 tablespoons plus ½ teaspoon vegetable oil, divided
1 cup all-purpose flour
⅔ cup yellow cornmeal
⅓ cup whole wheat flour
2 teaspoons baking powder
½ teaspoon salt
¼ teaspoon ground red pepper
2 tablespoons sugar
1 cup fresh corn cut from cob or frozen, thawed
1 cup skim milk
1 egg

Coat a 9-inch cast-iron skillet with ½ teaspoon oil. Place skillet in a 425° oven for 10 minutes.

Combine remaining 3 tablespoons oil, flour, and remaining 9 ingredients in a bowl, stirring well; pour mixture into skillet. Bake at 425° for 25 minutes or until a wooden pick inserted in center comes out clean; cut into wedges. Yield: 12 wedges.

PER WEDGE: 140 CALORIES (30% FROM FAT)
FAT 4.6G (SATURATED FAT 0.9G)
PROTEIN 3.7G   CARBOHYDRATE 21.7G
CHOLESTEROL 19MG   SODIUM 117MG

Did You Know?

The word succotash comes from an Indian word meaning "boiled kernels of corn." Although many versions of succotash exist, it generally contains corn, lima beans, and chopped sweet pepper.

STRAWBERRY SHORTCAKE

Turbinado sugar is a type of raw sugar that has a mild flavor somewhat like molasses. Feel free to substitute regular granulated sugar to sprinkle on the shortcakes before baking.

2 cups all-purpose flour
2 teaspoons baking powder
¼ teaspoon baking soda
¼ teaspoon salt
¼ cup sugar
3 tablespoons plus 1 teaspoon chilled
    margarine, cut into small pieces
¾ cup 1% low-fat buttermilk
1 egg white, lightly beaten
1½ teaspoons turbinado or granulated sugar
Strawberry Topping
½ cup thawed reduced-calorie frozen whipped
    topping
Fresh strawberries (optional)

Combine first 5 ingredients in a bowl; cut in margarine with a pastry blender until mixture resembles coarse meal. Add buttermilk; stir just until dry ingredients are moistened.

Turn dough out onto a heavily floured surface. Knead dough 5 or 6 times. Roll dough to ½-inch thickness; cut with a 3-inch biscuit cutter. Place on a baking sheet, and brush with egg white; sprinkle with sugar.

Bake at 450° for 12 minutes or until golden. Split biscuits; place bottom halves of biscuits on individual plates. Spoon ½ cup Strawberry Topping over each biscuit half; top with remaining half. Spoon 1 tablespoon whipped topping over each shortcake. Garnish with fresh strawberries, if desired. Yield: 8 servings.

STRAWBERRY TOPPING

4 cups sliced fresh strawberries
1 tablespoon sugar
¼ cup red currant jelly
2 tablespoons water

Combine strawberries and sugar; let stand 30 minutes. Combine jelly and water in a small saucepan; place over low heat. Cook, stirring constantly, until jelly melts. Remove from heat; stir in strawberry mixture. Spoon mixture into a bowl; cover and chill. Yield: 4 cups.

PER SERVING: 259 CALORIES (22% FROM FAT)
FAT 6.2G (SATURATED FAT 1.6G)
PROTEIN 4.9G   CARBOHYDRATE 46.8G
CHOLESTEROL 0MG   SODIUM 191MG

Strawberry Shortcake

Seasoned Alaskan Salmon, Poached Pineapple in Yukon Jack, Sourdough and Mushroom Strata, and Cranberry-Orange Cider

ALASKAN LIGHT

America's last frontier may be rugged territory, but its refined flavors make for a delightful supper or brunch menu. Fresh Alaskan salmon, sourdough bread, Yukon Jack (orange liqueur), and cranberries combine to make a meal as grand as the region itself.

For fun, write down little-known facts about Alaska, and give one to each guest. Let them share these while sampling the state's flavors.

Seasoned Alaskan Salmon

Sourdough and Mushroom Strata

Poached Pineapple in Yukon Jack

Cranberry-Orange Cider

Serves 4
TOTAL CALORIES PER SERVING: 609
(CALORIES FROM FAT: 14%)

SEASONED ALASKAN SALMON

1 (12-ounce) salmon fillet
¼ teaspoon cracked black pepper
⅛ teaspoon salt
⅛ teaspoon paprika
⅛ teaspoon ground red pepper
Vegetable cooking spray
⅓ cup thinly sliced shallots
1 ounce reduced-fat, low-salt ham, cut into
    ¼-inch-wide strips
¾ cup canned no-salt-added chicken broth,
    undiluted
1 tablespoon dark brown sugar
Fresh thyme sprigs (optional)

Cut salmon fillet into 4 equal pieces. Sprinkle cracked pepper, salt, paprika, and ground red pepper evenly over salmon pieces, and set salmon aside.

Coat a large nonstick skillet with cooking spray; place over medium-high heat until hot. Add shallots and ham; sauté 2 minutes or until shallots are tender.

Add salmon fillets to skillet; cook 4 minutes. Turn fillets, and cook 2 minutes; add broth and brown sugar. Bring to a boil; cook 4 minutes or until fish flakes easily when tested with a fork. Transfer fillets to individual serving plates. Spoon ham mixture evenly over fillets. Garnish with fresh thyme sprigs, if desired. Yield: 4 servings.

PER SERVING: 151 CALORIES (35% FROM FAT)
FAT 5.9G (SATURATED FAT 1.0G)
PROTEIN 18.5G   CARBOHYDRATE 4.4G
CHOLESTEROL 50MG   SODIUM 168MG

SOURDOUGH AND MUSHROOM STRATA

6 (1¾-ounce) sourdough rolls, divided
2 tablespoons grated Parmesan cheese
1 cup sliced fresh crimini mushrooms
1 cup sliced fresh shiitake mushrooms
¼ cup sliced green onions
⅓ cup canned no-salt-added chicken broth,
    undiluted
1 tablespoon finely chopped fresh thyme
2 cloves garlic, minced
Vegetable cooking spray
1 tablespoon all-purpose flour
1 cup skim milk
¼ cup frozen egg substitute, thawed
¼ teaspoon salt
¼ teaspoon freshly ground pepper

Tear 1 sourdough roll into small pieces. Position knife blade in food processor bowl; add sourdough roll pieces. Process until crumbs form. Combine 2 tablespoons breadcrumbs and Parmesan cheese in a large bowl, stirring well; set aside. Reserve remaining breadcrumbs for another use. Cut remaining 5 rolls into 1-inch cubes. Add bread cubes to breadcrumb mixture; set aside.

Combine crimini mushrooms and next 5 ingredients in a large nonstick skillet. Bring to a boil over medium-high heat. Cover, reduce heat, and simmer 5 minutes. Uncover and simmer 5 minutes or until liquid evaporates; remove from heat. Add mushroom mixture to bread mixture, tossing gently. Spoon bread mixture into a 1-quart baking dish coated with cooking spray, and set aside.

Combine flour and milk, stirring until smooth. Stir in egg substitute, salt, and pepper.

Pour milk mixture over bread mixture in baking dish. Cover and bake at 325° for 20 minutes. Uncover and bake 20 minutes or until set. Let stand 5 minutes before serving. Yield: 4 servings.

PER SERVING: 231 CALORIES (11% FROM FAT)
FAT 2.8G (SATURATED FAT 0.6G)
PROTEIN 13.8G   CARBOHYDRATE 38.8G
CHOLESTEROL 3MG   SODIUM 453MG

POACHED PINEAPPLE IN YUKON JACK

If Yukon Jack is unavailable, substitute Triple Sec or another orange-flavored liqueur.

1 small fresh pineapple, peeled and cored
3 tablespoons brown sugar
3 tablespoons Yukon Jack
2 tablespoons water
½ teaspoon grated orange rind
¼ cup fresh blueberries
¼ cup fresh raspberries

Cut pineapple into 12 (¼-inch-thick) slices, and set slices aside. Reserve remaining pineapple for another use.

Combine sugar, Yukon Jack, and water in a large nonstick skillet; cook, stirring constantly, over low heat until sugar dissolves. Add pineapple slices and orange rind; bring to a boil. Cover, reduce heat, and simmer 10 minutes, turning pineapple once.

Arrange 3 pineapple slices on each individual serving plate; top each serving with 1 tablespoon blueberries and 1 tablespoon raspberries. Drizzle syrup evenly over each serving. Yield: 4 servings.

PER SERVING: 84 CALORIES (5% FROM FAT)
FAT 0.5G (SATURATED FAT 0.0G)
PROTEIN 0.5G CARBOHYDRATE 21.3G
CHOLESTEROL 0MG SODIUM 4MG

CRANBERRY-ORANGE CIDER

You can also serve this cider over crushed ice for a cool, refreshing beverage.

4 cups water
2 cups fresh or frozen cranberries, thawed
6 whole cloves
2 (3-inch) sticks cinnamon
½ cup sugar
¼ cup frozen orange juice concentrate, thawed
2 tablespoons lemon juice

Combine first 4 ingredients in a medium saucepan; bring to a boil. Cover, reduce heat, and simmer 25 minutes; let cool. Pour mixture through a cheesecloth-lined wire-mesh strainer into a bowl; press with back of spoon against the sides of the strainer to squeeze out juice. Discard pulp, seeds, cloves, and cinnamon stick remaining in strainer.

Combine cranberry juice mixture, sugar, orange juice concentrate, and lemon juice in saucepan. Place over low heat, and cook, stirring constantly, until sugar dissolves. Yield: 4 (1-cup) servings.

PER SERVING: 143 CALORIES (1% FROM FAT)
FAT 0.1G (SATURATED FAT 0.0G)
PROTEIN 0.6G CARBOHYDRATE 36.7G
CHOLESTEROL 0MG SODIUM 1MG

Alcohol Substitutions

If you don't have the alcoholic beverage called for, you need not abandon the recipe. You can usually substitute another liquid (alcoholic or not) with satisfactory results.

For example, you may use Triple Sec instead of Yukon Jack as suggested above, or simply use 3 tablespoons orange juice.

Low-sodium chicken broth is often a suitable substitute for white wine. Likewise, low-sodium beef broth is a good substitute for red wine. In recipes where a fruity taste is desired, you can use white or red grape juice or apple juice instead of white or red wine.

Another possibility is to use flavored extracts, such as rum or brandy. A little extract goes a long way, so start with a small amount (1 teaspoon or less). If the amount of liquid is critical, you can add broth, juice, or water to the extract.

AN EVENING IN JAPAN

Invite some friends on a culinary trip to Japan. Start with Shrimp Mirin, a flavorful appetizer served with a rice wine sauce. Next, offer a bowl of Soba Noodles in Broth, followed by Beef Teriyaki, steamed rice (½ cup per serving), and Sesame Vegetable Medley. End the meal with Sweet Oranges with Berries and a cup of steaming green tea.

Shrimp Mirin

Soba Noodles in Broth

Beef Teriyaki

Steamed rice

Sesame Vegetable Medley

Sweet Oranges with Berries

Green tea

Serves 10
TOTAL CALORIES PER SERVING: 555
(CALORIES FROM FAT: 17%)

SHRIMP MIRIN

½ cup mirin (rice wine)
1 tablespoon sugar
1 tablespoon peeled, chopped gingerroot
3 tablespoons low-sodium soy sauce
1 teaspoon lemon juice
⅛ teaspoon salt
20 large fresh shrimp, peeled and deveined
2 tablespoons rice wine vinegar
1 tablespoon mirin
⅛ teaspoon salt
1½ cups shredded daikon (oriental radish)
Vegetable cooking spray
10 lemon slices
10 cucumber slices

Combine ½ cup mirin and next 5 ingredients. Reserve half of mirin mixture. Pour remaining half of mirin mixture into a large heavy-duty, zip-top plastic bag; add shrimp. Seal bag, and shake until shrimp are well coated. Marinate in refrigerator up to 4 hours, turning bag occasionally.

Combine vinegar, 1 tablespoon mirin, and ⅛ teaspoon salt in a bowl. Add daikon; toss gently.

Remove shrimp from marinade; discard marinade. Place shrimp on rack of a broiler pan coated with cooking spray. Broil shrimp 5½ inches from heat (with electric oven door partially opened) 3 to 4 minutes on each side or until shrimp turn pink.

Place 1 lemon slice and 1 cucumber slice on each plate. Top each with daikon mixture and 2 shrimp.

Bring reserved half of mirin mixture to a boil in a saucepan. Pour into small bowls. Serve warm with shrimp. Yield: 10 appetizer servings.

Note: If mirin isn't available, substitute sherry. Add 2 additional teaspoons of sugar if you use the sherry.

PER SERVING: 44 CALORIES (8% FROM FAT)
FAT 0.4G (SATURATED FAT 0.1G)
PROTEIN 6.6G   CARBOHYDRATE 2.3G
CHOLESTEROL 60MG   SODIUM 195MG

Beef Teriyaki and Sesame Vegetable Medley

SOBA NOODLES IN BROTH

Look for soba noodles at Oriental markets. If unavailable, substitute spaghetti noodles.

3½ cups canned low-sodium chicken broth, undiluted
¼ pound skinned, boned chicken breast halves
2 stalks celery, cut into 2-inch pieces
1 small onion, quartered
1 carrot, cut into 2-inch pieces
3 quarts water
6 ounces soba (buckwheat) noodles, uncooked
2 tablespoons sugar
2½ tablespoons low-sodium soy sauce
1 tablespoon tahini
½ teaspoon pepper
¼ teaspoon salt
¼ pound fresh spinach, trimmed and chopped
2 tablespoons sliced green onions

Combine first 5 ingredients in a saucepan; bring to a boil. Cover, reduce heat, and simmer 20 minutes. Remove chicken; set aside. Discard celery, onion, and carrot. Skim fat from broth, and set broth aside.

Bring 3 quarts water to a boil in a Dutch oven; add noodles. Reduce heat; simmer, uncovered, 5 to 7 minutes or until tender. Drain; set aside.

Shred chicken; return to broth. Add noodles, sugar, and next 5 ingredients; cook over medium heat 2 minutes, stirring frequently. Ladle into soup bowls; sprinkle with green onions. Yield: 10 (½-cup) servings.

PER SERVING: 107 CALORIES (16% FROM FAT)
FAT 1.9G (SATURATED FAT 0.2G)
PROTEIN 6.9G   CARBOHYDRATE 16.8G
CHOLESTEROL 8MG   SODIUM 221MG

BEEF TERIYAKI

¾ cup dry sherry
¾ cup low-sodium soy sauce
1 tablespoon vegetable oil
½ teaspoon dry mustard
⅛ teaspoon onion powder
3 cloves garlic, minced
2 pounds boneless top sirloin steak (1 inch thick)
1½ tablespoons dark corn syrup
1 tablespoon water
2 teaspoons cornstarch
Vegetable cooking spray
1 tablespoon plus 2 teaspoons dry mustard
1 tablespoon water
Green onion fans (optional)

Combine first 6 ingredients, stirring well. Reserve ½ cup sherry mixture. Pour remaining sherry mixture into a large heavy-duty, zip-top plastic bag. Add steak; seal bag, and shake until steak is well coated. Marinate in refrigerator up to 4 hours, turning bag occasionally.

Combine reserved sherry mixture, corn syrup, 1 tablespoon water, and cornstarch in a small saucepan, stirring well. Bring to a boil over medium-low heat, and cook, stirring constantly, 1 minute. Remove from heat. Set sherry mixture aside, and keep warm.

Remove steak from marinade, discarding marinade. Place steak on rack of broiler pan coated with cooking spray. Broil 5½ inches from heat (with electric oven door partially opened) 6 to 7 minutes on each side or to desired degree of doneness. Slice steak diagonally across grain into ¼-inch-thick slices. Arrange steak strips on individual serving plates. Brush cooked sherry mixture evenly over steak strips.

Combine 1 tablespoon plus 2 teaspoons mustard and 1 tablespoon water in a small bowl, stirring well with a wire whisk. Spoon mustard mixture evenly alongside steak strips. Garnish with green onion fans, if desired. Yield: 10 servings.

PER SERVING: 167 CALORIES (33% FROM FAT)
FAT 6.1G (SATURATED FAT 2.1G)
PROTEIN 22.5G   CARBOHYDRATE 3.5G
CHOLESTEROL 65MG   SODIUM 267MG

SESAME VEGETABLE MEDLEY

1 cup small fresh shiitake mushrooms
Vegetable cooking spray
2 teaspoons sesame oil
1 pound fresh snow pea pods, trimmed
1 cup diagonally sliced carrot
½ cup canned bamboo shoots, drained
1 clove garlic, minced
2 tablespoons water
1 tablespoon low-sodium soy sauce
2 teaspoons sugar
¼ teaspoon cornstarch
¼ teaspoon chicken-flavored bouillon granules
¼ teaspoon Dijon mustard
1 tablespoon sesame seeds, toasted

Remove and discard mushroom stems.

Coat a large nonstick skillet with cooking spray; add sesame oil. Place over medium-high heat until hot. Add mushroom caps, snow peas, and next 3 ingredients; sauté 2 to 3 minutes or until vegetables are crisp-tender.

Combine water and next 5 ingredients, and add to vegetable mixture. Cook, stirring constantly, until sauce is slightly thickened. Arrange evenly on individual serving plates, and sprinkle with sesame seeds. Yield: 10 (½-cup) servings.

PER SERVING: 64 CALORIES (23% FROM FAT)
FAT 1.6G (SATURATED FAT 0.2G)
PROTEIN 2.2G CARBOHYDRATE 10.0G
CHOLESTEROL 0MG   SODIUM 70MG

SWEET ORANGES WITH BERRIES

Honor your guests with this sweet creation. Oranges are considered a prized dessert in the Orient.

6 small oranges
¾ cup water
¾ cup rosé wine
½ cup sugar
2 whole cloves
2 (1-inch) slices peeled gingerroot
1 (2-inch) stick cinnamon
½ vanilla bean, split lengthwise
2 cups halved fresh strawberries

Peel oranges, removing pith. Cut oranges crosswise into ⅛-inch-thick slices. Remove and discard seeds. Set aside orange slices.

Combine water and next 6 ingredients in a medium saucepan; bring to a boil. Cover, reduce heat, and simmer 15 minutes. Pour mixture through a wire-mesh strainer. Add orange slices to hot syrup. Cover and chill.

Just before serving, stir in strawberries. Spoon fruit and liquid evenly into individual dessert dishes. Yield: 10 (½-cup) servings.

PER SERVING: 68 CALORIES (3% FROM FAT)
FAT 0.2G (SATURATED FAT 0.0G)
PROTEIN 0.6G CARBOHYDRATE 17.2G
CHOLESTEROL 0MG   SODIUM 2MG

Did You Know?

Nearly 4,000 years ago, the Chinese found that if they added tea leaves to the water they boiled to prevent sickness, it would improve the taste of the water. Then about 800 A.D., the Japanese discovered this, too.

In the Orient, green tea is popular. It has a greenish-yellow color and a slightly bitter flavor. Varied soils and climates yield a wide assortment of other types of tea as well.

Herbed Coq au Vin, Provençal-Style Tomatoes, and Salad Verte with Fresh Raspberries

CLASSIC FRENCH CUISINE

This classic French menu includes Herbed Coq au Vin served with a broiled tomato half and ½ cup baby carrots. Dessert features mounds of meringue atop chilled custard. Menu calories include a 6-ounce glass of wine and a 1-ounce slice of French bread per person.

Braised Artichokes with Sauce Béarnaise

Herbed Coq au Vin

Steamed baby carrots

Provençal-Style Tomatoes

Salad Verte with Fresh Raspberries

Commercial French bread

Almond Floating Islands

Red wine

Serves 6
TOTAL CALORIES PER SERVING: 775
(CALORIES FROM FAT: 16%)

BRAISED ARTICHOKES WITH SAUCE BÉARNAISE

1¼ cups plain nonfat yogurt
2 tablespoons reduced-calorie mayonnaise
3 tablespoons white wine vinegar
1 tablespoon minced green onions
2 cloves garlic, minced
¼ teaspoon pepper
1½ teaspoons minced fresh tarragon
6 medium artichokes (about 2¼ pounds)
Lemon wedge
1 large sweet yellow pepper, cut into thin strips

Line a colander or sieve with a double layer of cheesecloth; extend over edge of colander.

Stir yogurt until well blended. Pour into colander, and fold edges of cheesecloth over to cover yogurt. Place colander in a bowl to drain; chill 8 hours. Remove yogurt from colander; discard liquid in bowl. Remove yogurt from cheesecloth.

Combine drained yogurt and mayonnaise; set aside. Combine vinegar and next 3 ingredients in a saucepan; bring to a boil. Reduce heat, and simmer until mixture is reduced by half. Strain, reserving liquid; cool. Combine yogurt mixture, vinegar mixture, and tarragon; cover and chill.

Wash artichokes in cold water. Cut off stem end; trim about ½ inch from top of each artichoke. Remove any loose bottom leaves. Trim away about one-fourth of each outer leaf. Rub top and edges with lemon wedge to prevent discoloration.

Place artichokes in a Dutch oven; add water to a depth of 1 inch. Bring to a boil; cover, reduce heat, and simmer 25 minutes. Drain; let cool. Spread leaves apart; scrape out fuzzy thistle center (choke) with a spoon. Place artichokes on serving plates. Arrange pepper strips on plates. Serve with chilled yogurt sauce. Yield: 6 servings.

PER SERVING: 82 CALORIES (19% FROM FAT)
FAT 1.7G (SATURATED FAT 0.1G)
PROTEIN 4.9G   CARBOHYDRATE 13.5G
CHOLESTEROL 3MG   SODIUM 129MG

HERBED COQ AU VIN

6 (6-ounce) skinned chicken breast halves
3 tablespoons all-purpose flour
24 small pearl onions
Vegetable cooking spray
24 small fresh mushrooms
1 tablespoon olive oil
2 tablespoons cognac
3 ounces lean cooked ham, cut into thin strips
2 cups Pinot Noir or other dry red wine
1 cup water
2 cloves garlic, minced
1 teaspoon sugar
1 teaspoon beef-flavored bouillon granules
¼ teaspoon pepper
⅛ teaspoon freshly grated nutmeg
Bouquet Garni

Dredge chicken in flour; set aside.

Blanch onions in boiling water 1 minute; drain and pat dry with paper towels. Coat a large Dutch oven with cooking spray; place over medium-high heat until hot. Add blanched onions and mushrooms; sauté until tender. Remove from pan; set mixture aside.

Coat pan with cooking spray; add oil. Place over medium-high heat until hot. Add chicken; cook 4 minutes on each side or until chicken is browned. Pour cognac over chicken; ignite with a long-stemmed match. When flames die, stir in ham and remaining 8 ingredients. Bring to a boil; reduce heat, and simmer 30 minutes.

Add reserved onions and mushrooms; simmer 30 additional minutes or until chicken is tender. Transfer chicken to a serving platter, using a slotted spoon. Discard Bouquet Garni. Cook sauce mixture over high heat 15 minutes or until reduced to a glaze; spoon over chicken. Yield: 6 servings.

BOUQUET GARNI

6 fresh parsley sprigs
6 fresh thyme sprigs
2 fresh rosemary sprigs
2 (4-inch) pieces celery

Place half of herbs in hollow of each celery piece. Place celery pieces together, hollow side in, and secure with cotton string. Yield: 1 Bouquet Garni.

PER SERVING: 210 CALORIES (21% FROM FAT)
FAT 5.0G (SATURATED FAT 1.0G)
PROTEIN 30.3G   CARBOHYDRATE 9.8G
CHOLESTEROL 74MG   SODIUM 441MG

PROVENÇAL-STYLE TOMATOES

3 medium tomatoes, halved crosswise
1 teaspoon olive oil
Vegetable cooking spray
3 cloves garlic, minced
¼ cup fine, dry breadcrumbs
2 tablespoons chopped fresh parsley
1 teaspoon chopped fresh thyme
1 teaspoon sugar
¼ teaspoon salt
¼ teaspoon pepper

Place tomatoes, cut side up, on an ungreased baking sheet. Brush cut side of tomatoes with oil; set aside.

Coat a small nonstick skillet with cooking spray; place over medium-high heat until hot. Add garlic, and sauté until tender. Stir in breadcrumbs and remaining 5 ingredients. Sprinkle breadcrumb mixture evenly over tomatoes. Broil 3 inches from heat (with electric oven door partially opened) 3 to 4 minutes or until lightly browned. Serve immediately. Yield: 6 servings.

PER SERVING: 50 CALORIES (25% FROM FAT)
FAT 1.4G (SATURATED FAT 0.2G)
PROTEIN 1.5G   CARBOHYDRATE 9.0G
CHOLESTEROL 0MG   SODIUM 146MG

SALAD VERTE WITH FRESH RASPBERRIES

¼ cup raspberry vinegar
2 tablespoons balsamic vinegar
2½ tablespoons reduced-calorie mayonnaise
2 teaspoons white wine Worcestershire sauce
2 cups torn curly endive
2 cups torn Boston or Bibb lettuce
2 cups torn romaine lettuce
1 cup fresh raspberries

Combine first 4 ingredients in a small bowl; stir with a wire whisk until blended. Set aside.

Combine salad greens in a large bowl; add vinegar mixture, and toss well. Add raspberries; toss lightly. Arrange on individual salad plates. Yield: 6 (1-cup) servings.

PER SERVING: 36 CALORIES (48% FROM FAT)
FAT 1.9G (SATURATED FAT 0.0G)
PROTEIN 0.8G   CARBOHYDRATE 4.9G
CHOLESTEROL 2MG   SODIUM 67MG

ALMOND FLOATING ISLANDS

3 cups skim milk
2 eggs, lightly beaten
½ cup sugar, divided
2 tablespoons plus 1 teaspoon cornstarch
1 teaspoon almond extract
2 egg whites
2 tablespoons finely chopped toasted almonds

Heat milk in a medium saucepan to simmering; set aside.

Combine eggs, ¼ cup plus 2 tablespoons sugar, and cornstarch in top of a double boiler; beat with a wire whisk until blended. Gradually stir about one-fourth of hot milk into egg mixture; add remaining hot milk, stirring constantly.

Bring water to a boil; reduce heat to low, and cook, stirring constantly, 12 to 15 minutes or until mixture coats a metal spoon. Remove from heat,

and stir in almond extract. Let cool; cover and chill thoroughly.

Beat egg whites at high speed of an electric mixer until soft peaks form. Gradually add remaining 2 tablespoons sugar, 1 tablespoon at a time, beating until stiff peaks form. Fold in almonds.

Pour boiling water into a 13- x 9- x 2-inch baking pan to a depth of 1 inch. Drop egg white mixture in 6 equal portions into boiling water. Bake at 350° for 15 to 18 minutes or until lightly browned. Carefully remove islands with a slotted spoon; drain on paper towels. Chill until ready to serve.

Spoon custard mixture into 6 individual dessert dishes; top each with an island. Serve immediately. Yield: 6 servings.

PER SERVING: 165 CALORIES (17% FROM FAT)
FAT 3.1G (SATURATED FAT 0.8G)
PROTEIN 7.9G   CARBOHYDRATE 26.2G
CHOLESTEROL 73MG   SODIUM 103MG

Fat Alert

As delectable as French food is, it has the reputation of being high in calories and loaded with fat. But by making a few modifications, you can enjoy the best of French cuisine and still stay within your low-fat diet plans.

Prepare the classic béarnaise sauce on page 25 with reduced-calorie mayonnaise and nonfat yogurt instead of heavy cream. Keep the fat low in Almond Floating Islands by using skim milk instead of whole.

For other low-fat French specialties, try Coquilles St. Jacques à la Provençale (page 86), Roasted Ratatouille (page 115), Soufflé aux Épinards (page 117), Lean French Bread (page 64), and Pear Galette (page 134).

Fresh Tomato and Cheese Pizza (recipe on page 42)

ETHNIC PARTY FOODS

*T*hrowing a theme party has never been easier. In the following pages, you'll find the ingredients for Chinese, Greek, Italian, and Mexican fare. Use these recipes as appetizers, or combine three or more for a complete meal.

You may want to plan a Chinese dim sum party. Born in Cantonese tea houses, dim sum is a style of eating: a bit of this, a bit of that—as with the foods offered on page 30 and following. Or host a Greek celebration, and serve Mediterranean Bean Dip, Spinach-Feta Rolls, and Stuffed Grape Leaves (pages 33 and 34).

For an Italian evening, go with crostini, panini, and calzones (pages 36, 38, and 39). We've also included four versions of "Americanized" Italian pizza—one with a traditional yeast dough crust and three that use convenience products for preparation ease.

Baked Chicken and Vegetable Egg Rolls

2 (4-ounce) skinned, boned chicken breast
    halves, cut into small pieces
1 (10-ounce) package frozen chopped broccoli,
    thawed and well drained
½ cup chopped canned water chestnuts
¼ cup sliced green onions
2 cloves garlic, minced
¼ cup low-sodium soy sauce, divided
Vegetable cooking spray
1 egg white
12 egg roll wrappers
¼ cup canned low-sodium chicken broth,
    undiluted
2 tablespoons minced green onions
1 teaspoon sesame oil

Position knife blade in food processor bowl; add
chicken, broccoli, water chestnuts, ¼ cup green
onions, garlic, and 1 tablespoon soy sauce. Process
5 seconds.

Coat a large nonstick skillet with cooking spray,
and place over medium-high heat until hot. Add
chicken mixture, and cook 5 to 6 minutes or until
chicken is done, stirring frequently. Remove from
heat, and let cool. Stir in egg white.

Mound 2 heaping tablespoons chicken mixture
in center of each egg roll wrapper. Fold top corner
of each wrapper over filling; then fold left and right
corners over filling. Lightly brush exposed corner
of wrappers with water. Tightly roll filled end of
wrapper toward exposed corner; gently press corner
to seal securely. Coat both sides of egg roll with
cooking spray.

Place egg rolls on a baking sheet coated with
cooking spray. Bake at 450° for 6 to 7 minutes on
each side or until golden brown.

Combine remaining 3 tablespoons soy sauce,
chicken broth, 2 tablespoons green onions, and oil
in a small bowl; stir well. Serve 1½ teaspoons sauce
with each egg roll. Yield: 12 appetizers.

Per Appetizer: 71 Calories (16% from Fat)
Fat 1.3g (Saturated Fat 0.2g)
Protein 6.3g Carbohydrate 8.0g
Cholesterol 12mg Sodium 200mg

Steamed Pearl Balls

*Lining the bamboo steamer with steamed cabbage
leaves keeps the rice balls from sticking.*

½ cup uncooked long-grain rice
½ pound ground chicken or turkey
½ cup finely chopped mushrooms
½ cup minced green onions
1 tablespoon low-sodium soy sauce
2 teaspoons cornstarch
1 teaspoon peeled, minced gingerroot
½ teaspoon sugar
½ teaspoon dark sesame oil
Steamed green cabbage leaves

Place rice in a bowl; cover with water to 1 inch
above rice, and let stand 1 hour. Drain rice well;
place rice in a shallow dish, and set aside.

Combine chicken and next 7 ingredients in a
large bowl; stir well. Drop chicken mixture by
rounded tablespoons into rice, rolling to form rice-
coated balls.

Line a bamboo steamer with steamed cabbage
leaves. Place balls ½ inch apart in steamer; cover
with steamer lid. Add water to a large skillet to
depth of 1 inch; bring to a boil. Place steamer in
skillet, and steam balls 20 minutes or until rice is
tender. Remove balls from steamer. Yield: 14
appetizers.

Per Appetizer: 55 Calories (25% from Fat)
Fat 1.5g (Saturated Fat 0.4g)
Protein 3.8g Carbohydrate 6.3g
Cholesterol 12mg Sodium 46mg

Dim Sum Delights

In Chinese dim sum tea parlors, carts
loaded with a variety of finger foods are
wheeled around to tables where customers
select what they'd like to eat. Delicacies in a
dim sum feast may include pearl balls, pot
stickers, and tiny egg rolls, along with piquant
sauces, such as the Hot Mustard Sauce on
page 33, that are used for dipping.

Steamed Pearl Balls

Chicken Pot Stickers with Hot Mustard Sauce

CHICKEN POT STICKERS

2 teaspoons vegetable oil
2 cups finely chopped green cabbage
½ cup water
½ pound ground chicken or turkey
⅓ cup minced green onions
1 tablespoon peeled, minced gingerroot
½ teaspoon salt
½ teaspoon dark sesame oil
1 egg white
1 clove garlic, crushed
30 wonton wrappers
2 teaspoons cornstarch
1 tablespoon plus 1 teaspoon vegetable oil, divided
1 cup water, divided
Hot Mustard Sauce

Heat 2 teaspoons vegetable oil in a large nonstick skillet over medium-high heat. Add cabbage; cook 9 minutes or until lightly browned, stirring frequently. While cabbage cooks, add ½ cup water, 1 tablespoon at a time, to keep cabbage from sticking to pan. Spoon cabbage into a medium bowl; let cool completely. Add chicken and next 6 ingredients to cabbage; stir well.

Working with 1 wonton wrapper at a time (cover remaining wonton wrappers to keep them from drying out), spoon about 1 tablespoon chicken mixture into the center of each wrapper.

Moisten edges of wrapper with water, and bring 2 opposite corners to center, pinching points to seal. Bring the remaining 2 corners to center, pinching points to seal. Pinch 4 edges together to seal. Place pot stickers on a large baking sheet sprinkled with cornstarch; cover loosely with a towel to keep them from drying out.

Heat 2 teaspoons vegetable oil in a nonstick skillet over medium heat. Place half of pot stickers in skillet; cook 3 minutes or until bottoms are lightly browned. Add ½ cup water to skillet; cover and cook 3 minutes or until liquid is absorbed. Place on a serving platter; set aside, and keep warm.

Wipe skillet with a paper towel. Repeat procedure with remaining 2 teaspoons vegetable oil, remaining pot stickers, and remaining ½ cup water. Serve with Hot Mustard Sauce. Yield: 30 appetizers.

HOT MUSTARD SAUCE
3 tablespoons dry mustard
3 tablespoons water
1½ teaspoons rice vinegar
¼ teaspoon salt

Combine all ingredients in a small bowl, and stir with a wire whisk until blended. Let stand 10 minutes. Yield: ¼ cup.

PER APPETIZER: 47 CALORIES (31% FROM FAT)
FAT 1.6G (SATURATED FAT 0.3G)
PROTEIN 2.6G CARBOHYDRATE 5.3G
CHOLESTEROL 7MG SODIUM 114MG

MINIATURE EGG FOO YUNG

Egg substitute keeps both fat and cholesterol to a minimum in this Oriental dish.

¾ cup frozen egg substitute, thawed
1 (8-ounce) package frozen cooked salad shrimp, thawed and drained
½ cup chopped canned water chestnuts
½ cup chopped canned bean sprouts
¼ cup chopped green onions
1 teaspoon peeled, minced gingerroot
¼ teaspoon salt
¼ teaspoon hot sauce
Vegetable cooking spray
3 tablespoons plus 2 teaspoons Chinese hot mustard

Beat egg substitute with a wire whisk until foamy. Stir in shrimp and next 6 ingredients.

Coat a nonstick griddle with cooking spray; preheat to 350°. For each pancake, spoon 1 tablespoon shrimp mixture onto hot griddle. Cook 2 to 3 minutes or until browned on bottom; turn and cook 2 to 3 additional minutes or until browned. Transfer to a serving platter. Top each pancake with ½ teaspoon hot mustard. Serve immediately. Yield: 22 appetizers.

Note: You may top the egg foo yung pancakes with Hot Mustard Sauce (at left) instead of Chinese hot mustard.

PER APPETIZER: 20 CALORIES (18% FROM FAT)
FAT 0.4G (SATURATED FAT 0.0G)
PROTEIN 2.9G CARBOHYDRATE 1.1G
CHOLESTEROL 16MG SODIUM 84MG

MEDITERRANEAN BEAN DIP

1 (15½-ounce) can Great Northern beans, drained
1 tablespoon chopped fresh parsley
1 tablespoon lemon juice
2 teaspoons olive oil
1 teaspoon anchovy paste
½ teaspoon dried Italian seasoning
1 small clove garlic
6 drops of hot sauce

Place all ingredients in container of an electric blender or food processor; cover and process until smooth. Spoon mixture into a bowl, and stir well. Serve with raw vegetables or unsalted crackers. Yield: 1¼ cups.

PER TABLESPOON: 21 CALORIES (21% FROM FAT)
FAT 0.5G (SATURATED FAT 0.1G)
PROTEIN 1.2G CARBOHYDRATE 3.0G
CHOLESTEROL 0MG SODIUM 71MG

SPINACH-FETA ROLLS

1 (10-ounce) package fresh spinach
Butter-flavored vegetable cooking spray
½ cup minced onion
⅓ cup light ricotta cheese
¼ cup crumbled feta cheese
1 tablespoon dry white wine
½ teaspoon dried oregano
¼ teaspoon salt
¼ teaspoon garlic powder
¼ teaspoon pepper
18 sheets commercial frozen phyllo pastry,
   thawed

Trim and chop spinach; place in a large sauce-pan. Add water to pan to depth of 2 inches; bring to a boil. Cook just until spinach wilts, stirring occasionally. Drain well; press spinach between paper towels until barely moist.

Coat a nonstick skillet with cooking spray. Place over medium-high heat until hot. Add onion, and sauté until tender. Add spinach, ricotta cheese, and next 6 ingredients; stir well. Set aside.

Place 1 sheet of phyllo on a damp towel (cover remaining phyllo sheets to keep them from drying out). Lightly coat phyllo with cooking spray. Top with another phyllo sheet; lightly coat with cooking spray. Cut stack of phyllo crosswise into 5 strips (each about 3¼ inches wide).

Working with 1 strip at a time, place 2 teaspoons spinach mixture at base of strip (keeping remaining strips covered). Fold lengthwise edges in about ½ inch, and roll up, jellyroll fashion. Place rolls, seam side down, on ungreased baking sheets. (Keep rolls covered before baking.) Repeat procedure with remaining phyllo and spinach mixture. Coat rolls with cooking spray, and bake at 375° for 15 minutes or until golden. Yield: 45 appetizers.

PER APPETIZER: 30 CALORIES (27% FROM FAT)
FAT 0.9G (SATURATED FAT 0.2G)
PROTEIN 1.0G   CARBOHYDRATE 4.5G
CHOLESTEROL 1MG   SODIUM 63MG

STUFFED GRAPE LEAVES

1 cup plain low-fat yogurt
3 tablespoons chopped fresh mint or
   1 tablespoon dried mint, divided
1 teaspoon grated lemon rind
1 teaspoon honey
30 large bottled grape leaves
2 tablespoons olive oil
1¾ cups finely chopped onion
1 clove garlic, minced
¼ cup fresh lemon juice, divided
2 cups cooked rice (cooked without salt or fat)
½ cup dried currants
⅓ cup pine nuts, toasted
1 tablespoon chopped fresh dill or 1 teaspoon
   dried dillweed
½ teaspoon salt
¼ teaspoon pepper
1 (15-ounce) can chick-peas (garbanzo beans),
   rinsed and drained
Vegetable cooking spray

Combine yogurt, 2 tablespoons fresh mint, lemon rind, and honey in a bowl; stir well. Cover and chill.

Rinse grape leaves under cold water; drain and pat dry with paper towels. Remove stems; discard.

Heat oil in a large nonstick skillet over medium heat. Add chopped onion, and sauté 10 minutes. Add garlic, and sauté 1 minute. Remove from heat; stir in remaining 1 tablespoon fresh mint, 2 table-spoons lemon juice, rice, and next 6 ingredients.

Spoon 1 rounded tablespoon rice mixture onto center of each grape leaf. Bring 2 opposite points of leaf to center, and fold over filling. Beginning at short side, roll up leaf tightly, jellyroll fashion. Repeat procedure with remaining grape leaves.

Place stuffed grape leaves, seam side down, in a 13- x 9- x 2-inch baking dish coated with cooking spray. Drizzle remaining 2 tablespoons lemon juice over leaves. Cover and bake at 350° for 30 minutes or until thoroughly heated. Serve warm or chilled with 1½ teaspoons yogurt mixture per appetizer. Yield: 30 appetizers.

PER APPETIZER: 60 CALORIES (32% FROM FAT)
FAT 2.1G (SATURATED FAT 0.4G)
PROTEIN 1.9G   CARBOHYDRATE 9.2G
CHOLESTEROL 0MG   SODIUM 119MG

Greek Salad Hero

GREEK SALAD HEROS

¾ cup thinly sliced fresh mushrooms
½ cup thinly sliced cucumber
2 tablespoons sliced ripe olives
2 tablespoons crumbled feta cheese
1 tablespoon white balsamic vinegar
⅛ teaspoon dried oregano
4 cherry tomatoes, thinly sliced
1 clove garlic, minced
2 (2½-ounce) submarine rolls
2 green leaf lettuce leaves
2 ounces thinly sliced reduced-fat, low-salt
   ham
2 ounces thinly sliced cooked turkey breast

Combine first 8 ingredients in a small bowl; toss gently. Let stand 30 minutes, tossing occasionally.

Cut a thin slice lengthwise off top of each roll; set tops aside. Cut a 2-inch-wide, V-shaped wedge down length of the bottom part of each roll. Reserve bread wedges for another use.

Drain vegetable mixture. Line each roll with a lettuce leaf; top evenly with ham and turkey. Spoon vegetable mixture evenly over meat; cover with bread tops. Yield: 2 servings.

PER SERVING: 345 CALORIES (31% FROM FAT)
FAT 12.0G (SATURATED FAT 3.1G)
PROTEIN 20.7G CARBOHYDRATE 39.3G
CHOLESTEROL 58MG SODIUM 730MG

ROASTED SWEET PEPPER AND OLIVE CROSTINI

1 pound sweet red peppers, roasted and peeled
   (about 2 large)
1 pound sweet yellow peppers, roasted and
   peeled (about 2 large)
⅓ cup sliced green olives
⅓ cup sliced ripe olives
1 tablespoon drained capers
1 teaspoon olive oil
⅛ teaspoon pepper
32 (½-inch-thick) diagonally cut slices French
   bread baguette, toasted

Cut peppers into 1- x ¼-inch julienne strips. Combine pepper strips, green olives, and next 4 ingredients in a bowl, and stir well. Cover and let stand at room temperature for 2 hours.

Spoon about 1 tablespoon pepper mixture onto each bread slice. Yield: 32 appetizers.

Note: Refer to page 101 for instructions on roasting peppers.

PER APPETIZER: 29 CALORIES (19% FROM FAT)
FAT 0.6G (SATURATED FAT 0.1G)
PROTEIN 0.8G   CARBOHYDRATE 5.1G
CHOLESTEROL 0MG   SODIUM 85MG

Roasted Sweet Pepper and Olive Crostini

Bruschetta

BRUSCHETTA

Vegetable cooking spray
8 (¾-inch-thick) diagonally cut slices Italian
   bread (about 8 ounces)
1 clove garlic, halved
1 tablespoon plus 1 teaspoon extra-virgin
   olive oil
¼ teaspoon kosher salt
Parsley sprigs (optional)
Garlic cloves (optional)

Coat grill rack with cooking spray; place on grill over medium-hot coals (350° to 400°). Place bread slices on rack, and cook 2 minutes on each side or until lightly browned. Remove from grill.

Rub cut sides of garlic over one side of each bread slice, and brush with oil; sprinkle with salt. If desired, garnish with parsley sprigs and garlic cloves. Yield: 8 appetizers.

Note: Broil bread slices 2 minutes on each side instead of grilling, if desired.

PER APPETIZER: 99 CALORIES (24% FROM FAT)
FAT 2.6G (SATURATED FAT 0.3G)
PROTEIN 2.6G CARBOHYDRATE 16.1G
CHOLESTEROL 0MG SODIUM 203MG

Prosciutto and Fontina Panini

PROSCIUTTO AND FONTINA PANINI

1 (5.25-ounce) package focaccia (Italian
    flat bread) or 1 (8-ounce) package Italian
    cheese-flavored pizza crust (such as
    Boboli)
8 very thin slices prosciutto (about 2 ounces)
¼ cup (1 ounce) shredded fontina cheese
1 cup trimmed arugula or watercress
2 (⅛-inch-thick) slices purple onion, separated
    into rings
2 teaspoons balsamic vinegar
⅛ teaspoon pepper
Black olives (optional)

Slice each bread round in half horizontally.
Divide prosciutto between bottom halves of bread,
and top each bread half with fontina cheese,
arugula, and onion slices. Drizzle vinegar over sandwiches, and sprinkle with pepper; cover with top
halves of bread. Wrap sandwiches tightly in aluminum foil; bake at 300° for 15 minutes. Garnish
with black olives, if desired. Yield: 2 servings.

PER SERVING: 330 CALORIES (31% FROM FAT)
FAT 11.5G (SATURATED FAT 5.6G)
PROTEIN 20.2G   CARBOHYDRATE 40.3G
CHOLESTEROL 33MG   SODIUM 846MG

PORK AND TOMATILLO CALZONES

1 (1-pound) loaf commercial frozen white
   bread dough
¾ pound tomatillos
½ pound pork tenderloin
½ teaspoon dried thyme
¼ teaspoon pepper
Vegetable cooking spray
½ cup finely chopped onion
2 cloves garlic, minced
¼ cup chopped fresh cilantro
¼ teaspoon salt
¼ teaspoon dried oregano
¼ teaspoon ground cumin
3 tablespoons canned diced green chiles
2 teaspoons lemon juice

Thaw bread dough.

Discard husks and stems from tomatillos. Place in a saucepan; add water to cover. Bring to a boil; cook 8 minutes or until tender. Drain and set aside.

Trim fat from pork, and dice. Sprinkle with thyme and pepper. Coat a medium saucepan with cooking spray; place over medium-high heat until hot. Add onion and garlic; sauté until tender. Add pork; sauté until browned. Add tomatillos, cilantro, and remaining 5 ingredients. Bring to a boil; reduce heat to medium, and cook 10 minutes or until mixture is reduced to 2 cups. Remove from heat.

Divide dough into 8 equal portions. Working with 1 portion at a time (cover remaining portions to keep dough from drying out), roll to ⅛-inch thickness. Place on a baking sheet coated with cooking spray; pat each portion into a 6-inch circle with floured fingertips. Spoon ¼ cup pork mixture onto half of each circle; moisten edges of dough with water. Fold dough over filling; press edges together with a fork to seal. Coat with cooking spray.

Bake at 375° for 20 minutes or until golden. Remove from oven, and lightly coat again with cooking spray. Serve warm. Yield: 8 servings.

PER SERVING: 180 CALORIES (14% FROM FAT)
FAT 2.8G (SATURATED FAT 0.3G)
PROTEIN 11.2G   CARBOHYDRATE 27.8G
CHOLESTEROL 18MG   SODIUM 353MG

HAMBURGER-MUSHROOM PIZZA

This family favorite can be assembled and baked in less than 30 minutes.

1 (16-ounce) loaf unsliced Italian bread
½ cup commercial pizza sauce
8 (⅛-inch-thick) slices onion, separated into
   rings
1 cup presliced fresh mushrooms
6 ounces ground round
1 teaspoon dried Italian seasoning
½ teaspoon garlic powder
¼ teaspoon dried crushed red pepper
1½ cups (6 ounces) preshredded pizza
   double-cheese (a blend of part-skim
   mozzarella and Cheddar cheeses)

Cut bread loaf in half horizontally. Place both halves of bread, cut side up, on a large baking sheet. Spread ¼ cup pizza sauce over each bread half. Divide onion rings and mushrooms evenly between bread halves. Crumble beef into ½-inch pieces, and divide beef evenly between bread halves. Sprinkle Italian seasoning, garlic powder, and red pepper evenly over each pizza; top each with ¾ cup cheese.

Bake at 500° for 9 minutes or until beef is done and cheese melts. Cut each half into 3 equal pieces. Yield: 6 servings.

PER SERVING: 301 CALORIES (29% FROM FAT)
FAT 9.7G (SATURATED FAT 2.7G)
PROTEIN 15.1G   CARBOHYDRATE 35.4G
CHOLESTEROL 31MG   SODIUM 542MG

SICILIAN PIZZA

A plum tomato is small, pear-shaped, and full of flavor. Roma is one of the most popular varieties of plum tomatoes.

1 package active dry yeast
¼ cup warm water (105° to 115°)
1 teaspoon sugar
2 teaspoons olive oil
2 cups all-purpose flour
1 cup whole wheat flour
¼ teaspoon salt
¾ cup lukewarm water (95° to 100°)
Vegetable cooking spray
1 tablespoon all-purpose flour
6 ounces lean ground chicken
¾ teaspoon fennel seeds, crushed
¼ teaspoon salt
1 cup seeded, chopped plum tomato
4 ounces fresh mushrooms, thinly sliced
1½ tablespoons chopped fresh oregano
¾ cup (3 ounces) shredded part-skim
       mozzarella cheese
½ cup (2 ounces) freshly grated Parmesan
       cheese

Combine yeast and ¼ cup warm water in a 1-cup liquid measuring cup; add sugar, and let stand 5 minutes. Add oil.

Position knife blade in food processor bowl; add yeast mixture, 2 cups all-purpose flour, whole wheat flour, and ¼ teaspoon salt. Process 30 seconds, stopping once to scrape down sides. Pour ¾ cup lukewarm water through food chute with processor running; process until blended and dough is soft.

Turn dough out onto a work surface, and knead until smooth (about 2 minutes). Place in a large bowl coated with cooking spray, turning to coat top. Cover and let rise in a warm place (85°), free from drafts, 45 minutes or until doubled in bulk.

Punch dough down. Sprinkle 1 tablespoon all-purpose flour over work surface. Turn dough out onto floured surface, and knead lightly 4 or 5 times; roll into a 15- x 10-inch rectangle. Place dough in a 15- x 10- x 1-inch jellyroll pan coated with cooking spray.

Cover and let rise in a warm place, free from drafts, 30 minutes or until doubled in bulk. Coat dough with cooking spray. Bake at 450° for 10 minutes; set aside.

Coat a large nonstick skillet with cooking spray, and place over medium-high heat until hot. Add chicken, fennel seeds, and ¼ teaspoon salt; cook, stirring constantly, until chicken is done. Drain.

Sprinkle tomato evenly over crust, leaving a ½-inch border. Spread chicken mixture evenly over tomato. Arrange mushrooms over chicken mixture; sprinkle oregano and cheeses evenly over pizza. Bake at 450° for 10 minutes or until crust is lightly browned. Yield: 8 servings.

PER SERVING: 278 CALORIES (20% FROM FAT)
FAT 6.2G (SATURATED FAT 2.7G)
PROTEIN 16.9G CARBOHYDRATE 39.1G
CHOLESTEROL 26MG SODIUM 327MG

ROASTED VEGETABLE PIZZA

Roasting the vegetables adds a robust flavor to this healthy pizza.

1 (10-ounce) can refrigerated pizza crust
       dough
Vegetable cooking spray
1 tablespoon minced fresh thyme or
       1 teaspoon dried thyme
2 tablespoons balsamic vinegar
1 teaspoon olive oil
¼ teaspoon salt
4 cloves garlic, thinly sliced
4 small red potatoes, each cut into 8 wedges
1 small yellow squash, cut into ¼-inch slices
1 small sweet red pepper, cut into 2-inch pieces
1 small sweet onion, cut into 12 wedges
1¼ cups (5 ounces) shredded sharp provolone
       cheese
Thyme sprig (optional)

Unroll pizza dough onto a large baking sheet coated with cooking spray; fold under edges of dough to form an 11-inch circle. Bake pizza crust at

Roasted Vegetable Pizza

425° for 7 minutes, and set crust aside.

Combine thyme and next 8 ingredients in a bowl; toss well. Place vegetable mixture in a 13- x 9- x 2-inch baking dish. Bake at 500° for 15 minutes, stirring halfway through cooking time.

Reduce oven temperature to 425°. Sprinkle half of cheese over prepared pizza crust. Arrange roasted vegetables over cheese; top with remaining half of cheese. Bake at 425° for 12 minutes or until crust is lightly browned. Let stand 5 minutes before cutting. Garnish with thyme sprig, if desired. Yield: 6 servings.

PER SERVING: 293 CALORIES (27% FROM FAT)
FAT 8.8G (SATURATED FAT 4.2G)
PROTEIN 10.0G   CARBOHYDRATE 40.2G
CHOLESTEROL 16MG   SODIUM 539MG

FRESH TOMATO AND CHEESE PIZZA

(pictured on page 28)

2 thin slices purple onion, cut in half
2 cloves garlic, thinly sliced
Olive oil-flavored vegetable cooking spray
1 (10-ounce) can refrigerated pizza crust
    dough
1 teaspoon olive oil
1 (15-ounce) carton part-skim ricotta cheese
½ cup (2 ounces) shredded part-skim
    mozzarella cheese
½ cup freshly grated Parmesan cheese,
    divided
1 tablespoon chopped fresh basil
4 plum tomatoes, cut into ¼-inch-thick slices
3 yellow tomatoes, cut into ¼-inch-thick slices
3 red teardrop tomatoes, cut in half
8 sprigs fresh basil (optional)

Place onion and garlic on a baking sheet coated
with cooking spray. Coat onion and garlic with
cooking spray. Broil 5½ inches from heat (with
electric oven door partially opened) 8 to 10 minutes
or until charred; set aside.

Shape pizza crust dough into a ball; gently press
into a 4-inch circle on a baking sheet coated with
cooking spray. Roll dough into a 12-inch circle.

Cut 1-inch-deep slits around edge of dough at ½-
inch intervals; fold every other ½-inch-wide piece
of dough in toward center. Brush with oil.

Combine ricotta cheese, mozzarella cheese, ¼
cup Parmesan cheese, and chopped basil, stirring
well. Spread cheese mixture over pizza dough,
leaving a ½-inch border. Arrange tomato slices over
cheese mixture; top with roasted onion and garlic.
Sprinkle with remaining ¼ cup Parmesan cheese.

Bake at 500° on bottom rack of oven for 12 minutes or until crust is browned. Transfer pizza to a
cutting board; top with teardrop tomato halves.
Garnish with basil sprigs, if desired. Let stand 5
minutes before cutting. Yield: 6 servings.

PER SERVING: 266 CALORIES (28% FROM FAT)
FAT 8.4G (SATURATED FAT 4.1G)
PROTEIN 17.9G CARBOHYDRATE 32.3G
CHOLESTEROL 21MG SODIUM 491MG

TEX-MEX BLACK BEAN DIP

1 (15-ounce) can black beans, rinsed and
    drained
1 teaspoon vegetable oil
½ cup chopped onion
2 cloves garlic, minced
½ cup diced tomato
⅓ cup mild picante sauce
½ teaspoon ground cumin
½ teaspoon chili powder
¼ cup (1 ounce) shredded reduced-fat
    Monterey Jack cheese
¼ cup chopped fresh cilantro
1 tablespoon fresh lime juice
Cilantro sprig (optional)

Place beans in a bowl; partially mash until
chunky. Set aside.

Heat oil in a medium nonstick skillet over
medium heat. Add onion and garlic; sauté 4 minutes or until tender. Add beans, tomato, and next 3

Tex-Mex Black Bean Dip

ingredients; cook, stirring constantly, 5 minutes or until thickened. Remove from heat; add cheese, cilantro, and lime juice, stirring until cheese melts. Garnish with cilantro sprig, if desired. Serve warm or at room temperature with fat-free tortilla chips. Yield: 1⅔ cups.

PER TABLESPOON: 21 CALORIES (21% FROM FAT)
FAT 0.5G (SATURATED FAT 0.2G)
PROTEIN 1.3G CARBOHYDRATE 3.1G
CHOLESTEROL 1MG SODIUM 68MG

QUICK AND EASY GAZPACHO

2¼ cups peeled, coarsely chopped tomato
    (about 1 pound)
1½ cups no-salt-added tomato juice
¾ cup peeled, seeded, and diced cucumber
¼ cup chopped fresh parsley
2 tablespoons minced fresh onion
1 tablespoon balsamic vinegar
½ teaspoon ground cumin
½ teaspoon minced fresh jalapeño pepper
⅛ teaspoon salt
⅛ teaspoon coarsely ground pepper
1 small clove garlic, minced
Fresh parsley sprigs (optional)

Combine first 11 ingredients in container of an electric blender; cover and process until chunky. Pour mixture into a bowl; cover and chill. Ladle into soup bowls, and garnish with parsley sprigs, if desired. Yield: 4 (1-cup) servings.

PER SERVING: 49 CALORIES (9% FROM FAT)
FAT 0.5G (SATURATED FAT 0.1G)
PROTEIN 2.2G CARBOHYDRATE 11.3G
CHOLESTEROL 0MG SODIUM 97MG

CHICKEN-RICE BURRITOS

(pictured on cover)

Ground red pepper (optional)
8 (6-inch) flour tortillas
Vegetable cooking spray
½ pound skinned, boned chicken breast, cut
    into ¼-inch strips
¼ cup chopped onion
2 tablespoons minced jalapeño pepper
½ teaspoon chili powder
⅛ teaspoon salt
⅛ teaspoon ground cumin
2 cloves garlic, minced
¼ cup water
2 teaspoons cornstarch
1½ cups cooked brown rice (cooked without
    salt or fat)
1 cup (4 ounces) shredded reduced-fat
    Cheddar cheese
½ cup chopped tomato
½ cup peeled, chopped cucumber
¼ cup chopped fresh cilantro
½ cup mild salsa
1 cup nonfat sour cream
Cilantro sprigs (optional)

Sprinkle red pepper evenly over tortillas, if desired; rub in with fingertips. Wrap tortillas in aluminum foil, and heat at 325° for 15 minutes.

Coat a large nonstick skillet with cooking spray; place over medium-high heat until hot. Add chicken and next 6 ingredients; cook 3 minutes or until chicken is done. Combine water and cornstarch; stir well, and add to chicken mixture in skillet. Bring to a boil; cook, stirring constantly, 1 minute or until thickened. Combine chicken mixture and rice; stir well. Spoon ¼ cup mixture down center of each tortilla; top each with 2 tablespoons cheese, 1 tablespoon tomato, 1 tablespoon cucumber, and 1½ teaspoons cilantro. Fold sides over; top each with 1 tablespoon salsa and 2 tablespoons sour cream. If desired, garnish with cilantro sprigs and ground red pepper. Yield: 8 servings.

PER SERVING: 279 CALORIES (22% FROM FAT)
FAT 6.7G (SATURATED FAT 2.3G)
PROTEIN 19.6G CARBOHYDRATE 33.5G
CHOLESTEROL 33MG SODIUM 397MG

HOT-AND-SPICY PORK BURRITOS

¼ cup lime juice
2½ tablespoons dried crushed red pepper
1 tablespoon chili powder
1 tablespoon hot chili powder
1½ teaspoons dried oregano
1 teaspoon ground cumin
½ teaspoon garlic powder
¼ teaspoon salt
¼ teaspoon ground red pepper (optional)
1 (10½-ounce) can low-sodium chicken broth
2 pounds lean, boneless center-cut loin pork chops (⅓ inch thick)
16 (6-inch) flour tortillas
2 cups shredded lettuce
1 (8-ounce) carton plain nonfat yogurt

Combine first 10 ingredients in a 13- x 9- x 2-inch baking dish; stir well. Trim fat from chops. Add chops to marinade, turning to coat. Cover and marinate in refrigerator 8 hours, turning occasionally.

Bake chops in marinade, covered, at 325° for 1 hour, basting occasionally with marinade. Uncover and bake 1 additional hour or until most of liquid is absorbed and meat is saucy. Let cool slightly, and shred meat.

Spoon 3½ tablespoons shredded pork down center of each tortilla. Roll up tortillas, and secure with wooden picks, if necessary. Place 2 tortillas on each plate, and top with ¼ cup shredded lettuce and 1 tablespoon yogurt. Yield: 8 servings.

Note: Shredded pork freezes well. To freeze in 2-serving portions, divide shredded pork evenly among 4 labeled heavy-duty, zip-top plastic bags or airtight containers. Freeze up to 3 months.

To heat for 2 servings, thaw 1 (2-serving) bag in refrigerator or microwave oven. Cook pork in a nonstick skillet over medium heat 4 minutes or until thoroughly heated, stirring frequently; add 2 tablespoons water, if necessary. Assemble burritos as indicated above.

PER SERVING: 193 CALORIES (29% FROM FAT)
FAT 6.3G (SATURATED FAT 1.7G)
PROTEIN 16.0G CARBOHYDRATE 17.2G
CHOLESTEROL 36MG SODIUM 227MG

BLACK BEAN EMPANADITAS

Empanar is Spanish for "to bake in pastry." Empanaditas are tiny ravioli-size pastries.

Vegetable cooking spray
3 ounces lean ground pork
2 tablespoons finely chopped onion
1½ tablespoons finely chopped sweet red pepper
1 small clove garlic, minced
⅓ cup drained canned black beans
2 tablespoons no-salt-added tomato sauce
1 tablespoon dry red wine
1½ teaspoons chopped fresh cilantro
⅛ teaspoon ground cumin
⅛ teaspoon ground allspice
1 (10-ounce) package refrigerated pizza crust

Coat a large nonstick skillet with cooking spray; add ground pork and next 3 ingredients. Cook over medium heat until meat is browned, stirring until it crumbles. Drain and pat dry with paper towels. Wipe drippings from skillet with a paper towel.

Return pork mixture to skillet. Add black beans and next 5 ingredients. Cook over medium-high heat 8 to 10 minutes or until liquid is absorbed, stirring frequently. Remove from heat.

Roll pizza crust into a 13-inch square. Cut with a 3½-inch round biscuit cutter; place on baking sheets coated with cooking spray.

Place 1 tablespoon bean mixture in center of each circle. Fold dough over bean mixture to form half-circles. Seal edges of dough securely by pressing with a fork. Spray tops of empanaditas with cooking spray.

Bake at 375° for 15 to 18 minutes or until lightly browned. Serve warm. Yield: 1 dozen.

PER APPETIZER: 75 CALORIES (24% FROM FAT)
FAT 2.0G (SATURATED FAT 0.5G)
PROTEIN 3.9G CARBOHYDRATE 10.5G
CHOLESTEROL 6MG SODIUM 159MG

Black Bean Empanaditas

Turkey Enchiladas

TURKEY ENCHILADAS

1 pound freshly ground raw turkey breast
2 cups no-salt-added salsa, divided
1 (10-ounce) package frozen chopped spinach,
     thawed and drained
1 (8-ounce) package nonfat cream cheese,
     cubed
12 (6-inch) corn tortillas
Vegetable cooking spray
1 (14½-ounce) can no-salt-added whole
     tomatoes, undrained and chopped
1 teaspoon ground cumin
¾ cup (3 ounces) shredded reduced-fat
     Cheddar cheese
3 cups shredded lettuce
¼ cup plus 2 tablespoons nonfat sour cream

Cook turkey in a large nonstick skillet over medium heat until browned, stirring until it crumbles. Add 1 cup salsa, spinach, and cream cheese. Cook until cheese melts, stirring frequently.

Remove turkey mixture from skillet; set aside.

Wipe skillet dry with a paper towel; place over medium heat until hot. Coat both sides of tortillas with cooking spray. Place 1 tortilla in skillet. Cook 15 seconds on each side. Spoon about ⅓ cup turkey mixture across center of tortilla. Roll up; place seam side down in a 13- x 9- x 2-inch baking dish coated with cooking spray. Repeat procedure with remaining tortillas and turkey mixture.

Combine remaining 1 cup salsa, tomatoes, and cumin; pour over tortillas. Bake, uncovered, at 350° for 25 to 30 minutes or until thoroughly heated. Sprinkle with shredded cheese, and let stand 2 minutes.

Place ½ cup lettuce on each individual serving plate. Arrange two enchiladas over lettuce on each plate. Top each serving with 1 tablespoon sour cream. Yield: 6 servings.

PER SERVING: 349 CALORIES (15% FROM FAT)
FAT 6.0G (SATURATED FAT 2.6G)
PROTEIN 34.2G CARBOHYDRATE 39.7G
CHOLESTEROL 63MG SODIUM 703MG

TURKEY FAJITAS

Two (4-ounce) boneless chicken breast halves may be substituted for the turkey cutlets.

½ pound turkey breast cutlets
2 tablespoons low-sodium soy sauce
1 tablespoon fresh lime juice
1 tablespoon water
2 teaspoons minced garlic
1 teaspoon olive oil
½ teaspoon cracked pepper
¼ teaspoon ground cumin
2 tablespoons chopped avocado
1 tablespoon tomatillo salsa
1 tablespoon low-fat sour cream
1 teaspoon minced onion
¾ teaspoon minced fresh cilantro
½ teaspoon minced jalapeño pepper
Olive oil-flavored vegetable cooking spray
1 cup thinly sliced sweet red pepper
½ cup thinly sliced onion
2 (8-inch) flour tortillas

Cut turkey into strips; place in a small shallow dish. Combine soy sauce and next 6 ingredients; pour over turkey. Cover and marinate in refrigerator 2 hours.

Place avocado in a small bowl, and mash; stir in salsa and next 4 ingredients. Set aside.

Remove turkey from marinade, discarding marinade. Coat a nonstick skillet with cooking spray; place over medium-high heat until hot. Add turkey; sauté 2 minutes. Add red pepper and onion; sauté 6 minutes or until turkey is done and vegetables are tender. Spoon mixture evenly down centers of tortillas. Roll up tortillas, folding in sides. Serve with avocado sauce. Yield: 2 servings.

PER SERVING: 343 CALORIES (24% FROM FAT)
FAT 9.3G (SATURATED FAT 2.1G)
PROTEIN 31.8G CARBOHYDRATE 31.3G
CHOLESTEROL 71MG SODIUM 498MG

CRABMEAT AND CORN QUESADILLAS

8 ounces fresh lump crabmeat, drained
½ cup fresh or frozen corn kernels, thawed
½ cup diced sweet red pepper
½ cup minced fresh cilantro
⅓ cup chopped green onions
¼ cup plus 1 tablespoon nonfat sour cream
1 teaspoon hot sauce
½ teaspoon ground cumin
10 (8-inch) flour tortillas
1¼ cups (5 ounces) shredded reduced-fat
    Monterey Jack cheese
Vegetable cooking spray

Combine first 8 ingredients in a medium bowl, stirring mixture well. Spoon crabmeat mixture evenly over 5 tortillas; spread to within ½ inch of edge. Sprinkle evenly with cheese, and top with remaining tortillas.

Coat a large nonstick skillet with cooking spray; place over medium-high heat until hot. Add quesadillas, one at a time, and cook 1 to 2 minutes on each side or until lightly browned and cheese melts. Cut each quesadilla into 4 wedges, and serve immediately. Yield: 20 appetizers.

PER APPETIZER: 92 CALORIES (27% FROM FAT)
FAT 2.8G (SATURATED FAT 1.0G)
PROTEIN 6.2G CARBOHYDRATE 10.4G
CHOLESTEROL 16MG SODIUM 158MG

PICADILLO TORTILLAS

½ pound ground round
1 cup peeled, finely chopped Rome apple
2 tablespoons raisins
1 tablespoon minced jalapeño pepper
½ teaspoon salt
¼ teaspoon ground cumin
⅛ teaspoon ground cinnamon
Dash of ground coriander
1 (8-ounce) can no-salt-added tomato sauce
1 clove garlic, minced
4 (8-inch) flour tortillas

Crumble beef into a 1-quart casserole. Micro-wave at HIGH 3 minutes or until browned, stirring after 1½ minutes; drain. Wipe drippings from casserole with a paper towel. Return beef to casse-role; add apple and next 8 ingredients, stirring well. Microwave at HIGH 8 minutes or until thickened, stirring every 3 minutes.

Spread ½ cup beef mixture down center of each tortilla; fold sides over, and place in an 11- x 7- x 1½-inch baking dish. Cover with heavy-duty plas-tic wrap, and vent. Microwave at HIGH 1 minute or until thoroughly heated. Yield: 4 servings.

PER SERVING: 286 CALORIES (22% FROM FAT)
FAT 6.9G (SATURATED FAT 1.8G)
PROTEIN 17.0G CARBOHYDRATE 38.7G
CHOLESTEROL 35MG SODIUM 557MG

The tortilla, which is made with either wheat or corn flour, resembles a very thin pancake.

Tortillas are wrapped around a variety of fillings to form burritos, enchiladas, fajitas, quesadillas, and tacos. Or they can serve as the base for tostadas or chalupas.

CHILI VEGETABLE TOSTADAS

Vegetable cooking spray
2 teaspoons olive oil
2 cups coarsely chopped sweet red pepper
1 cup chopped onion
2 tablespoons seeded, minced jalapeño pepper
1 tablespoon chili powder
2 teaspoons ground cumin
½ teaspoon dried oregano
1 (16-ounce) can pinto beans, drained
1 (14½-ounce) can no-salt-added stewed
     tomatoes, undrained
1 (15½-ounce) can golden hominy, drained
8 (6-inch) corn tortillas
4 cups shredded lettuce, divided
¾ cup (3 ounces) shredded reduced-fat sharp
     Cheddar cheese, divided
½ cup nonfat sour cream, divided
½ cup chopped tomato, divided
Fresh parsley sprigs (optional)

Coat a large nonstick skillet with cooking spray; add oil. Place over medium-high heat until hot. Add red pepper and next 5 ingredients; sauté until vegetables are tender.

Add beans and stewed tomatoes; stir well. Reduce heat, and simmer, stirring constantly, until most of liquid is absorbed. Mash beans slightly with a potato masher or wooden spoon.

Add hominy, and cook until mixture is heated. Set aside, and keep warm.

Place tortillas on a baking sheet coated with cooking spray. Bake at 350° for 6 minutes; turn tor-tillas, and bake 6 additional minutes or until crisp.

Place ½ cup shredded lettuce on each individual serving plate. Top each with a tortilla. Spoon bean mixture evenly over tortillas; sprinkle each with 1½ tablespoons cheese. Top each with 1 tablespoon sour cream, and sprinkle tostadas evenly with chopped tomato. Garnish with parsley sprigs, if desired. Yield: 8 servings.

PER SERVING: 224 CALORIES (19% FROM FAT)
FAT 4.7G (SATURATED FAT 1.5G)
PROTEIN 10.7G CARBOHYDRATE 36.3G
CHOLESTEROL 7MG SODIUM 321MG

Chili Vegetable Tostadas

Spiral Almond Challah (recipe on page 67)

TRADITIONAL BREADS

*B*e it challah in a Jewish home or fruit-topped apfelkuchen in Germany, the aroma of hot bread fresh from the oven comforts the soul.

In this collection of classic breads from across the globe, you can also gain comfort from the fact that the fat content is low because of ingredient selection and preparation methods. Yet each recipe is so flavorful that you won't need to add extra butter or margarine at the table.

Turn the page for Southwestern Blue Cornbread, the first of several quick breads. You'll also find scones, a breakfast pastry, and a variation of the classic Irish soda bread.

Next are recipes calling for yeast, including breadsticks, focaccia, and black bread. On pages 64 and 65 are two sweet yeast breads, one with German roots and one from Greece.

SOUTHWESTERN BLUE CORNBREAD

Vegetable cooking spray
1 cup finely chopped sweet red pepper
½ cup finely chopped onion
¼ cup minced jalapeño pepper
1⅓ cups blue cornmeal
⅔ cup all-purpose flour
1½ teaspoons baking powder
½ teaspoon baking soda
½ teaspoon salt
2 tablespoons sugar
1 cup nonfat buttermilk
⅓ cup evaporated skimmed milk
¼ cup frozen egg substitute, thawed
3 tablespoons reduced-calorie margarine, melted

Coat a nonstick skillet with cooking spray; place over medium-high heat until hot. Add chopped red pepper, onion, and jalapeño pepper; sauté until tender.

Combine cornmeal and next 5 ingredients in a large bowl; make a well in center of mixture.

Combine buttermilk and remaining 3 ingredients in a small bowl; add buttermilk mixture to cornmeal mixture, stirring just until dry ingredients are moistened. Stir in vegetable mixture.

Pour batter into a 9-inch square pan coated with cooking spray. Bake at 425° for 25 minutes or until golden. Cut into squares to serve. Yield: 9 squares.

Note: Blue corn flour may be substituted for blue cornmeal. When using corn flour, reduce buttermilk to ¾ cup; then prepare as directed.

PER SQUARE: 160 CALORIES (19% FROM FAT)
FAT 3.4G (SATURATED FAT 0.5G)
PROTEIN 5.1G   CARBOHYDRATE 28.3G
CHOLESTEROL 1MG   SODIUM 294MG

BAKED HUSH PUPPIES

Many Southerners cook hush puppies in a deep-fat fryer to serve with fried catfish. These are baked instead.

⅔ cup yellow cornmeal
⅔ cup all-purpose flour
2 teaspoons baking powder
½ teaspoon salt
½ teaspoon sugar
¼ teaspoon onion powder
¼ teaspoon garlic powder
⅛ teaspoon ground red pepper
½ cup evaporated skimmed milk
2 tablespoons vegetable oil
3 egg whites, lightly beaten
Vegetable cooking spray

Combine first 8 ingredients in a medium bowl; make a well in center of mixture. Combine milk, oil, and egg whites; add to cornmeal mixture, stirring just until dry ingredients are moistened.

Spoon batter evenly into miniature (1¾-inch) muffin pans coated with cooking spray, filling three-fourths full. Bake at 425° for 13 to 15 minutes or until lightly browned. Remove from pans immediately. Yield: 2 dozen.

PER HUSH PUPPY: 46 CALORIES (29% FROM FAT)
FAT 1.5G (SATURATED FAT 0.3G)
PROTEIN 1.5G   CARBOHYDRATE 6.5G
CHOLESTEROL 0MG   SODIUM 87MG

FYI

When you want an authentic Southwestern flavor in your baked goods, try using blue cornmeal. The rich tradition of the flavored corn started when native American tribes stored their blue corn in limestone caves. During storage, the corn took on the limestone flavor that is now a characteristic of the region's cuisine. Blue cornmeal has a coarser texture than blue corn flour, which is fine and powdery.

Baked Hush Puppies

After combining dry ingredients in a medium bowl, make a well in center of mixture to hold combined liquid ingredients.

Add liquid ingredients to dry ingredients, stirring just until moistened. Overmixing will cause tunnels and peaks to form.

Coat miniature muffin pans with cooking spray to prevent hush puppies from sticking. Fill pans three-fourths full with batter.

Confetti Scones

CONFETTI SCONES

2 cups all-purpose flour
1 tablespoon baking powder
¼ teaspoon baking soda
¼ teaspoon salt
1 tablespoon sugar
½ teaspoon grated orange rind
3 tablespoons margarine
½ cup diced dried mixed fruit
¾ cup nonfat buttermilk
1 tablespoon all-purpose flour
1 tablespoon skim milk
Vegetable cooking spray
2 teaspoons sugar

Combine first 6 ingredients in a medium bowl; cut in margarine with a pastry blender until mixture resembles coarse meal. Stir in dried fruit. Add buttermilk, stirring with a fork just until dry ingredients are moistened.

Sprinkle 1 tablespoon flour evenly over work surface. Turn dough out onto floured surface; knead 10 to 12 times. Roll dough into an 8-inch circle, and cut into 10 wedges. Brush evenly with skim milk. Transfer wedges to a baking sheet coated with cooking spray. Sprinkle evenly with 2 teaspoons sugar. Bake at 425° for 15 minutes or until golden. Serve warm. Yield: 10 scones.

PER SCONE: 161 CALORIES (21% FROM FAT)
FAT 3.8G (SATURATED FAT 0.8G)
PROTEIN 3.6G CARBOHYDRATE 28.4G
CHOLESTEROL 1MG SODIUM 153MG

TRADITIONAL SCOTTISH OAT SCONES

½ cup raisins
1 cup boiling water
1¼ cups regular oats, uncooked
1 cup all-purpose flour
1½ teaspoons baking powder
¼ teaspoon salt
⅓ cup sugar
¼ cup margarine, chilled and cut into small
   pieces
¼ cup skim milk
1 egg, lightly beaten
Vegetable cooking spray

Combine raisins and boiling water; let stand 10 minutes. Drain well; set aside.

Position knife blade in food processor bowl; add oats, and process until finely ground. Combine oats, flour, and next 3 ingredients in a medium bowl; cut in margarine with a pastry blender until mixture resembles coarse meal. Add raisins; toss well.

Combine milk and egg. Add to dry ingredients; stir just until dry ingredients are moistened. (Dough will be sticky.)

Turn dough out onto a lightly floured surface; with floured hands, knead 4 to 5 times. Divide dough in half; pat each half into a 7-inch circle on a baking sheet coated with cooking spray. Cut each circle into 6 wedges, cutting into but not through dough. Bake at 400° for 12 minutes or until golden. Serve warm. Yield: 1 dozen.

PER SCONE: 151 CALORIES (29% FROM FAT)
FAT 4.9G (SATURATED FAT 1.0G)
PROTEIN 3.3G CARBOHYDRATE 24.0G
CHOLESTEROL 18MG SODIUM 140MG

DATE AND WALNUT SAMBOUSEKS

Enjoy these "little turnovers" as a breakfast pastry or a light dessert.

1 cup chopped pitted dates
½ cup unsweetened orange juice
2 tablespoons finely chopped walnuts
1 teaspoon vanilla extract
½ teaspoon ground cinnamon
1 (7.5-ounce) can refrigerated biscuit dough
   (10 biscuits)
Vegetable cooking spray
1 egg, lightly beaten
1 tablespoon sesame seeds

Combine chopped dates and orange juice in a medium saucepan; cover and cook over low heat 15 minutes or until liquid is absorbed. Remove from heat, and mash dates with a fork until smooth. Stir in chopped walnuts, vanilla, and cinnamon.

Divide dough into 10 biscuits. Working with 1 biscuit at a time, pat each biscuit into a 4-inch circle. Spoon about 1 tablespoon date mixture onto half of each circle. Fold dough over filling, and press edges together with a fork to seal. Place filled pastries about 2 inches apart on a baking sheet coated with cooking spray. Brush beaten egg over pastries, and sprinkle with sesame seeds.

Bake pastries at 350° for 25 minutes or until lightly browned. Remove from pan, and let cool on a wire rack. Yield: 10 pastries.

PER PASTRY: 163 CALORIES (20% FROM FAT)
FAT 3.6G (SATURATED FAT 0.7G)
PROTEIN 3.9G CARBOHYDRATE 29.8G
CHOLESTEROL 22MG SODIUM 147MG

Did You Know?

Traditionally, scones were slightly sweet and biscuitlike. Triangular in shape, they were baked on griddles in ovenless kitchens in the rural village of Scone in 16th-century Scotland.

Today's versions of the scone can be either sweet or savory. They can be made in many different shapes and sizes and are almost always baked in the oven.

STEAMED BROWN BREAD WITH CURRANTS AND WALNUTS

Versions of this recipe have been around since the days of the Pilgrims.

½ cup all-purpose flour
½ cup whole wheat flour
½ cup yellow cornmeal
½ teaspoon baking soda
½ teaspoon salt
¾ teaspoon ground cinnamon
1 cup low-fat buttermilk
⅓ cup molasses
½ cup dried currants
2 tablespoons chopped walnuts
Vegetable cooking spray

Combine first 6 ingredients in a large bowl, and make a well in center of mixture. Combine buttermilk and molasses; stir well. Add to flour mixture, stirring just until moistened. Fold in currants and walnuts.

Spoon mixture into a 13-ounce coffee can coated with cooking spray. Cover with aluminum foil coated with cooking spray; secure foil with a rubber band. Place can in an electric slow cooker; add enough hot water to cooker to come halfway up sides of can. Cook, covered, on HIGH 2 hours and 50 minutes or until a wooden pick inserted in center comes out clean. Remove can from water. Let bread cool, covered, in can on a wire rack for 5 minutes. Remove bread from can, and let cool completely on wire rack. Cut bread into slices. Yield: 8 slices.

PER SLICE: 170 CALORIES (13% FROM FAT)
FAT 2.4G (SATURATED FAT 0.5G)
PROTEIN 4.4G   CARBOHYDRATE 34.5G
CHOLESTEROL 0MG   SODIUM 252MG

HAZELNUT TEA BREAD

Also called filberts, most hazelnuts come from Oregon and Washington.

⅓ cup hazelnuts (about 1¾ ounces)
1 cup coarsely shredded peeled pear (about 2 medium)
¾ cup sugar
3 tablespoons vegetable oil
½ teaspoon grated lemon rind
½ teaspoon vanilla extract
1 egg, lightly beaten
1 egg white, lightly beaten
1½ cups all-purpose flour
½ cup whole wheat flour
1¼ teaspoons baking powder
½ teaspoon baking soda
½ teaspoon salt
¾ teaspoon ground cinnamon
Baking spray with flour

Place hazelnuts on a baking sheet. Bake at 350° for 15 minutes, stirring once. Turn nuts out onto a towel. Roll up towel, and rub off skins. Chop nuts; set aside.

Combine pear and next 6 ingredients in a large bowl; stir well. Combine nuts, all-purpose flour, and next 5 ingredients; add to pear mixture, stirring just until moistened.

Spoon batter into an 8½- x 4½-inch loafpan coated with baking spray. Bake at 350° for 1 hour and 5 minutes or until a wooden pick inserted in center comes out clean. Let cool in pan 10 minutes on a wire rack; remove from pan, and let cool completely on wire rack. Yield: 16 slices.

PER SLICE: 153 CALORIES (30% FROM FAT)
FAT 5.1G (SATURATED FAT 0.7G)
PROTEIN 2.8G   CARBOHYDRATE 24.9G
CHOLESTEROL 14MG   SODIUM 121MG

IRISH WHEATEN BREAD

The secret to this tender bread is in your hands—don't overwork the dough, just lightly knead it.

2 cups all-purpose flour
2 cups whole wheat flour
1 teaspoon baking soda
1 teaspoon salt
2 tablespoons sugar
3 tablespoons chilled stick margarine, cut into
     small pieces
1⅓ cups low-fat buttermilk
2 egg whites
Vegetable cooking spray

Position knife blade in food processor bowl; add first 5 ingredients, and pulse until well blended. With processor running, drop margarine through food chute, and process 10 seconds.

Combine buttermilk and egg whites; stir well.

With processor running, pour buttermilk mixture through food chute, and process 20 seconds or until dough leaves sides of bowl and forms a ball. Turn dough out onto a lightly floured surface, and lightly knead about 10 times.

Pat dough into an 8-inch round cakepan coated with cooking spray, and cut a ¼-inch-deep X in top of dough. Bake at 375° for 45 minutes or until lightly browned. Remove bread from pan, and let cool completely on a wire rack. Cut bread into wedges. Yield: 12 wedges.

PER WEDGE: 184 CALORIES (17% FROM FAT)
FAT 3.5G (SATURATED FAT 0.7G)
PROTEIN 6.3G CARBOHYDRATE 32.7G
CHOLESTEROL 1MG   SODIUM 337MG

Irish Wheaten Bread

Crisp Armenian Thin Bread

CRISP ARMENIAN THIN BREAD

1 package active dry yeast
1 cup warm water (105° to 115°)
½ teaspoon salt
2¾ cups bread flour, divided
Vegetable cooking spray
1 egg white
1 tablespoon water
¼ cup freshly grated Parmesan cheese
¼ cup sesame seeds
1 tablespoon plus 1 teaspoon poppy seeds

Dissolve yeast in 1 cup warm water in a bowl; let stand 5 minutes. Stir in salt and 2¼ cups flour to form a soft dough. Turn out onto a lightly floured surface; knead until smooth and elastic, adding enough of remaining ½ cup flour, 1 tablespoon at a time, to keep dough from sticking to hands.

Place dough in a large bowl coated with cooking spray, turning to coat top. Cover and let rise in a warm place (85°), free from drafts, 1 hour or until doubled in bulk.

Punch dough down; divide into 4 equal portions. Working with 1 portion at a time (cover remaining portions), shape each portion into a ball, and then roll into an 11-inch paper-thin oval on a large baking sheet coated with cooking spray. Combine egg white and 1 tablespoon water; brush over dough. Combine cheese, sesame seeds, and poppy seeds. Sprinkle one-fourth cheese mixture over dough.

Bake at 400° for 12 minutes or until crisp and lightly browned. Cool completely on a wire rack. Repeat procedure with remaining 3 portions of dough, egg white mixture, and cheese mixture. Break each round into 6 pieces. Yield: 12 servings.

PER SERVING: 145 CALORIES (19% FROM FAT)
FAT 3.1G (SATURATED FAT 0.7G)
PROTEIN 5.7G   CARBOHYDRATE 23.3G
CHOLESTEROL 2MG   SODIUM 141MG

GRISSINI ANISE

Grissini, *the Italian word for breadsticks, refers to the thin, crisp breadsticks, not the soft, chewy ones.*

3½ cups bread flour
¾ teaspoon salt
2 tablespoons sugar
1 tablespoon plus 1 teaspoon anise seeds
1 package rapid-rise yeast
1 cup plus 2 tablespoons very warm water
   (120° to 130°)
1 tablespoon olive oil
1 tablespoon brandy
½ teaspoon vanilla extract
Vegetable cooking spray
1 teaspoon water
1 egg white, lightly beaten
2 tablespoons turbinado or granulated sugar

Position knife blade in food processor bowl; add first 5 ingredients. Pulse 6 times or until blended. With processor running, add very warm water and next 3 ingredients through food chute; process until dough leaves sides of bowl and forms a ball.

Turn dough out onto a lightly floured surface; knead lightly 5 times. Place dough in a large bowl coated with cooking spray, turning to coat top. Cover and let rise in a warm place (85°), free from drafts, 40 minutes or until doubled in bulk.

Punch dough down; turn out onto a floured surface. Roll dough into a 24- x 7-inch rectangle, and cut into 24 (1-inch-wide) strips; roll each strip into a 15-inch rope. Place ropes 1 inch apart on baking sheets coated with cooking spray. Cover and let rise in a warm place, free from drafts, 15 minutes or until puffy.

Combine 1 teaspoon water and egg white, and gently brush over breadsticks; sprinkle with turbinado sugar. Bake at 400° for 13 minutes or until golden. Remove from pans; let cool on wire racks. Yield: 24 breadsticks.

PER BREADSTICK: 90 CALORIES (10% FROM FAT)
FAT 1.0G (SATURATED FAT 0.1G)
PROTEIN 2.7G CARBOHYDRATE 16.9G
CHOLESTEROL 0MG SODIUM 76MG

ITALIAN-STYLE FLAT BREADS

1 package active dry yeast
1 cup warm water (105° to 115°)
1 cup whole wheat flour
2 tablespoons brown sugar
¼ cup skim milk
2 teaspoons margarine, melted
1 teaspoon vegetable oil
3 cups thinly sliced onion
1 teaspoon sugar
¾ teaspoon salt, divided
2¼ cups plus 3 tablespoons bread flour,
   divided
Vegetable cooking spray

Combine yeast and warm water in a 2-cup liquid measuring cup; let stand 5 minutes. Combine yeast mixture, whole wheat flour, and next 3 ingredients in a large bowl, stirring until mixture is smooth. Cover and chill overnight.

Heat oil in a large nonstick skillet over medium heat until hot. Add onion; sprinkle with 1 teaspoon sugar and ¼ teaspoon salt. Cook 10 to 12 minutes or until golden, stirring frequently. Set aside, and let cool.

Combine yeast mixture, remaining ½ teaspoon salt, and 2¼ cups bread flour; stir until blended. Sprinkle 1 tablespoon bread flour evenly over work surface; turn dough out onto floured surface, and knead until smooth and elastic (about 10 minutes). Sprinkle remaining 2 tablespoons bread flour over work surface. Spoon onion mixture over dough. Knead gently to incorporate onion mixture into dough. (Dough will be sticky.)

Divide dough into 14 equal portions. Press each portion into a 4½-inch round. Place on baking sheets coated with cooking spray. Poke holes in rounds at 1-inch intervals with handle of a wooden spoon. Let rise, uncovered, in a warm place (85°), free from drafts, 20 minutes. Bake at 375° for 20 minutes or until golden. Yield: 14 flat bread rounds.

PER ROUND: 145 CALORIES (10% FROM FAT)
FAT 1.6G (SATURATED FAT 0.3G)
PROTEIN 4.8G CARBOHYDRATE 28.3G
CHOLESTEROL 0MG SODIUM 137MG

Garlic-Rosemary Focaccia and variations

GARLIC-ROSEMARY FOCACCIA

Each of these variations adds a different flavor twist to the flat bread.

¾ cup plus 2 tablespoons water
2 tablespoons olive oil
2¼ cups bread flour, divided
1 teaspoon salt
1 package rapid-rise yeast
1 tablespoon bread flour
Olive oil-flavored vegetable cooking spray
1 tablespoon cornmeal
1½ tablespoons commercial minced garlic
2 teaspoons chopped fresh rosemary

Combine water and oil in a saucepan; heat to 120° to 130°. Combine 1 cup bread flour, salt, and yeast in a large mixing bowl, stirring well. Gradually add liquid mixture to flour mixture, beating well at low speed of an electric mixer. Beat 2 additional minutes at medium speed. Gradually add ¾ cup flour; beat 2 minutes at medium speed. Gradually stir in enough of the remaining ½ cup flour to make a soft dough.

Sprinkle 1 tablespoon flour evenly over work surface. Turn dough out onto floured surface, and knead until smooth and elastic (about 10 minutes). Cover dough; let rest 10 minutes.

Coat a 14-inch round pizza pan with cooking spray; sprinkle pan with cornmeal. Set aside.

Punch dough down; turn out onto work surface, and knead lightly 4 or 5 times. Roll into a 14-inch circle. Place in prepared pan. Poke holes in dough at 1-inch intervals with handle of a wooden spoon.

Cover and let rise in a warm place (85°), free from drafts, 30 minutes or until doubled in bulk. Coat top of dough with cooking spray. Sprinkle garlic and rosemary evenly over dough. Bake at 375° for 25 to 30 minutes or until golden. Cut into wedges. Yield: 14 wedges.

PER WEDGE: 106 CALORIES (20% FROM FAT)
FAT 2.4G (SATURATED FAT 0.3G)
PROTEIN 3.1G   CARBOHYDRATE 17.6G
CHOLESTEROL 0MG   SODIUM 168MG

MOZZARELLA AND SUN-DRIED TOMATO FOCACCIA

Combine 1 cup sun-dried tomatoes (packed without oil) and 1 cup hot water in a small bowl; cover and let stand 15 minutes. Drain; chop tomatoes, and set aside.

Prepare dough as directed, omitting garlic and rosemary. After second rising, bake at 375° for 10 minutes. Remove bread from oven, and coat with cooking spray. Sprinkle tomato over dough. Return to oven, and bake 10 minutes. Sprinkle with ¼ cup plus 2 tablespoons (1½ ounces) shredded part-skim mozzarella cheese and ¼ cup shredded fresh basil. Bake 5 additional minutes or until cheese melts and bread is golden. Cut into wedges. Yield: 14 wedges.

PER WEDGE: 120 CALORIES (23% FROM FAT)
FAT 3.0G (SATURATED FAT 0.6G)
PROTEIN 4.2G   CARBOHYDRATE 19.2G
CHOLESTEROL 2MG   SODIUM 256MG

ONION FOCACCIA

Coat a large nonstick skillet with cooking spray; add 1 teaspoon olive oil. Place over medium-high heat until hot. Add 1 cup sliced sweet onion and 1 cup sliced purple onion, separated into rings; sauté until tender. Set sautéed onion rings aside.

Prepare dough as directed, omitting garlic and rosemary. After second rising, coat dough with cooking spray. Arrange sautéed onion rings over dough. Bake as directed. Cut into wedges. Yield: 14 wedges.

PER WEDGE: 114 CALORIES (22% FROM FAT)
FAT 2.8G (SATURATED FAT 0.4G)
PROTEIN 3.2G   CARBOHYDRATE 18.8G
CHOLESTEROL 0MG   SODIUM 168MG

FYI

Years before the first pizza, Italians were baking focaccia on the stone hearths of their homes. As time went on, toppings were added to this flat bread, and pizza was born.

ANADAMA BREAD

This bread originated in early New England.

1 package active dry yeast
¼ cup maple syrup
1 cup warm water (105° to 115°)
3¼ cups all-purpose flour, divided
½ cup yellow cornmeal
1 tablespoon vegetable oil
1 teaspoon salt
Vegetable cooking spray
2 teaspoons water
1 egg white

Dissolve yeast and maple syrup in 1 cup warm water in a large bowl; let stand 5 minutes. Add 2 cups flour, cornmeal, oil, and salt; beat at medium speed of an electric mixer until blended. Stir in ¾ cup flour to form a soft dough, and turn out onto a lightly floured surface. Knead until smooth and elastic (about 8 minutes); add enough of remaining ½ cup flour, 1 tablespoon at a time, to prevent dough from sticking to hands.

Place dough in a large bowl coated with cooking spray, turning to coat top. Cover and let rise in a warm place (85°), free from drafts, 1 hour or until doubled in bulk. Punch dough down, and roll into a 14- x 7-inch rectangle on a lightly floured surface. Roll up tightly, starting at short side, pressing firmly to eliminate air pockets; pinch seam and ends to seal. Place roll, seam side down, in an 8½- x 4½-inch loafpan coated with cooking spray. Cover and let rise 1 hour or until doubled in bulk.

Combine 2 teaspoons water and egg white, and gently brush over dough. Bake at 375° for 35 minutes or until loaf sounds hollow when tapped. Remove from pan; let cool on a wire rack. Yield: 16 slices.

PER SLICE: 125 CALORIES (9% FROM FAT)
FAT 1.2G (SATURATED FAT 0.2G)
PROTEIN 3.2G CARBOHYDRATE 24.9G
CHOLESTEROL 0MG SODIUM 152MG

RUSSIAN BLACK BREAD

2 packages active dry yeast
1½ cups warm water (105° to 115°), divided
1 tablespoon plus 1 teaspoon instant coffee granules
1 tablespoon honey
2 teaspoons margarine, melted
2½ cups plus 2 tablespoons bread flour, divided
2½ tablespoons unsweetened cocoa
1 tablespoon anise seeds
1½ teaspoons caraway seeds
¾ teaspoon salt
1 cup plus 1 tablespoon rye flour
Vegetable cooking spray
2 teaspoons cornmeal
1 egg white
1 tablespoon water

Combine yeast and 1 cup warm water in a 2-cup liquid measuring cup; let stand 5 minutes.

Combine coffee granules and remaining ½ cup warm water; stir until granules dissolve. Stir in honey and margarine. Combine yeast mixture, coffee mixture, 2½ cups plus 1 tablespoon bread flour, and next 4 ingredients in a mixing bowl; beat at medium speed of an electric mixer until well blended. Stir in enough of the rye flour to make a soft dough.

Sprinkle remaining 1 tablespoon bread flour over work surface. Turn dough out onto floured surface, and knead until smooth and elastic. Place dough in a large bowl coated with cooking spray, turning to coat top. Cover and let rise in a warm place (85°), free from drafts, 35 minutes or until doubled in bulk.

Sprinkle cornmeal over a baking sheet; set aside. Punch dough down; shape into a 6-inch round loaf. Place loaf on prepared baking sheet. Cover and let rise in a warm place, free from drafts, 30 minutes or until doubled in bulk. Cut a ½-inch-deep X in top of dough. Combine egg white and 1 tablespoon water; brush over loaf. Bake at 375° for 25 minutes or until loaf sounds hollow when tapped. Remove from baking sheet; cool on a wire rack. Cut into wedges. Yield: 18 wedges.

PER WEDGE: 112 CALORIES (9% FROM FAT)
FAT 1.1G (SATURATED FAT 0.2G)
PROTEIN 3.7G CARBOHYDRATE 21.4G
CHOLESTEROL 0MG SODIUM 107MG

Russian Black Bread

LEAN FRENCH BREAD

2¾ cups bread flour, divided
1 teaspoon salt
1 teaspoon sugar
1 package active dry yeast
1 cup very warm water (120° to 130°)
2 tablespoons bread flour, divided
Vegetable cooking spray
1 egg white, lightly beaten

Combine 1½ cups flour, salt, sugar, and yeast; stir. Gradually add water to flour mixture, beating at low speed of an electric mixer. Beat 2 additional minutes at medium speed. Stir in enough of remaining 1¼ cups flour to make a soft dough.

Sprinkle 1 tablespoon flour over work surface. Turn dough out; knead until smooth and elastic. Place in a bowl coated with cooking spray, turning to coat top. Cover; let rise in a warm place (85°), free from drafts, 1 hour or until doubled in bulk.

Sprinkle remaining 1 tablespoon flour over work surface. Punch dough down; turn out onto floured surface, and knead 4 or 5 times. Divide dough in half. Roll 1 portion of dough into a 15- x 7-inch rectangle. Roll up dough, starting at long side, pressing firmly to eliminate air pockets; pinch seam and ends to seal. Repeat with remaining dough.

Place loaves, seam side down, in 2 French baguette pans coated with cooking spray. Cover; let rise in a warm place, free from drafts, 30 minutes or until doubled in bulk. Cut ¼-inch-deep slits diagonally across loaves. Brush with egg white.

Place a shallow pan containing 1 inch of water on bottom rack of oven; place baguette pans on top rack. Bake at 400° for 20 minutes or until loaves are golden. Yield: 28 (1-inch) slices.

PER SLICE: 52 CALORIES (5% FROM FAT)
FAT 0.3G (SATURATED FAT 0.0G)
PROTEIN 1.9G CARBOHYDRATE 10.4G
CHOLESTEROL 0MG SODIUM 86MG

GERMAN SWEET BREAD

1 package active dry yeast
¼ cup sugar, divided
¾ cup warm water (105° to 115°)
2½ cups bread flour, divided
½ cup currants
⅓ cup instant nonfat dry milk powder
1 teaspoon grated lemon rind
½ teaspoon salt
¼ cup margarine, melted
1 egg
2 egg whites
Vegetable cooking spray
½ cup sifted powdered sugar
1½ teaspoons skim milk
¼ teaspoon vanilla extract
1 tablespoon sliced almonds, toasted

Dissolve yeast and 1 tablespoon sugar in warm water in a large bowl; let stand 5 minutes. Add remaining 3 tablespoons sugar, 1¼ cups flour, currants, and next 6 ingredients; beat at medium speed of an electric mixer until blended. Gradually stir in remaining 1¼ cups flour.

Coat a 1½-quart soufflé dish with cooking spray; spoon batter into dish. Cover and let rise in a warm place (85°), free from drafts, 25 to 30 minutes or until batter is ½ inch from top of soufflé dish.

Bake at 350° for 25 to 30 minutes or until a wooden pick inserted in center comes out clean. Cool in dish 10 minutes; remove from dish, and let cool on a wire rack.

Combine powdered sugar, milk, and vanilla; stir well. Drizzle mixture over top of cooled bread; sprinkle with almonds. Yield: 22 servings.

PER SERVING: 119 CALORIES (22% FROM FAT)
FAT 2.9G (SATURATED FAT 0.5G)
PROTEIN 3.5G CARBOHYDRATE 20.1G
CHOLESTEROL 10MG SODIUM 97MG

GRECIAN SWEET EGG BRAID

¾ cup 1% low-fat milk
3 bay leaves
2 packages active dry yeast
¾ cup plus 2 teaspoons sugar, divided
1 cup warm water (105° to 115°)
7½ cups bread flour, divided
½ cup margarine, softened
1½ teaspoons salt
1 egg
Vegetable cooking spray
¼ cup unsweetened apple juice
½ teaspoon cornstarch
1 teaspoon sesame seeds

Combine milk and bay leaves in a 2-cup glass measure, and microwave at HIGH 2½ minutes or until milk boils. Cover and let cool; discard bay leaves.

Dissolve yeast and 2 teaspoons sugar in warm water; let stand 5 minutes. Combine remaining ¾ cup sugar, 2 cups flour, margarine, salt, and egg in a large bowl. Add cooled milk and yeast mixture, and beat at medium speed of an electric mixer until blended. Gradually add 2 cups flour, and beat well. Add 3 cups flour, stirring until a soft dough forms.

Turn dough out onto a lightly floured surface. Knead until smooth and elastic (about 8 minutes); add enough remaining flour, 1 tablespoon at a time, to prevent dough from sticking to hands. Place dough in a large bowl coated with cooking spray, turning to coat top. Cover and let rise in a warm place (85°), free from drafts, 1 hour or until doubled in bulk.

Combine apple juice and cornstarch in a small saucepan; bring to a boil over medium-high heat, and cook, stirring constantly, 1 minute. Remove from heat; let cool completely.

Punch dough down, and turn out onto a lightly floured surface; let rest 5 minutes. Divide dough into 6 equal portions, shaping each portion into a 20-inch rope. Place 3 ropes lengthwise on half of a baking sheet coated with cooking spray (do not stretch); pinch ends together at one end to seal. Braid ropes; pinch loose ends to seal. Repeat procedure with remaining 3 ropes to make a second loaf.

Cover and let rise in a warm place 1 hour or until doubled in bulk.

Uncover dough; gently brush loaves with apple juice mixture, and sprinkle with sesame seeds. Bake at 350° for 30 minutes or until golden and the loaves sound hollow when tapped. Remove from pan; let cool on wire racks. Cut each loaf into 24 slices. Yield: 48 slices.

PER SLICE: 112 CALORIES (20% FROM FAT)
FAT 2.5G (SATURATED FAT 0.5G)
PROTEIN 3.0G CARBOHYDRATE 19.4G
CHOLESTEROL 5MG SODIUM 99MG

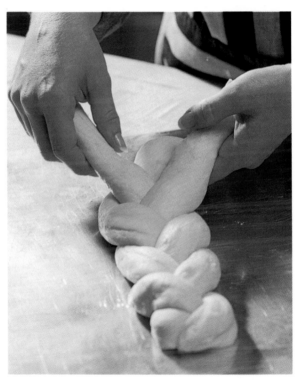

For each loaf, place 3 ropes of dough on a baking sheet; braid ropes, and pinch loose ends to seal.

Apfelkuchen

APFELKUCHEN

Apfelkuchen *means "apple cake" in German, but it's actually a yeast bread topped with a seasonal fruit.*

2½ cups plus 1 tablespoon all-purpose flour,
    divided
¼ teaspoon salt
¾ cup plus 3 tablespoons sugar, divided
1 package active dry yeast
½ cup very warm 1% low-fat milk (120° to
    130°)
¼ cup plus 1 tablespoon margarine, melted
    and divided
1 egg
Vegetable cooking spray
5 cups peeled, thinly sliced Granny Smith
    apples (about 1½ pounds)
1½ teaspoons lemon juice
2 tablespoons soft breadcrumbs
1 teaspoon ground cinnamon

Combine 1 cup flour, salt, 3 tablespoons sugar, and yeast in a large bowl; stir well. Add milk, 2 tablespoons margarine, and egg; beat at medium speed of an electric mixer 2 minutes or until smooth.

Stir in 1 cup plus 1 tablespoon flour to form a soft dough. Cover and let rise in a warm place (85°), free from drafts, 1 hour or until doubled in bulk.

Punch dough down. Spread evenly into a 15- x 10- x 1-inch jellyroll pan coated with cooking spray, using a spatula or fingers coated with cooking spray. Cover and let rise in a warm place, free from drafts, 30 minutes. (Dough will not double in bulk.)

Toss apples and lemon juice in a large bowl. Sprinkle with ¼ cup sugar, tossing to coat. Arrange apple slices in a single layer in 4 lengthwise rows on top of dough.

Combine remaining ½ cup flour, remaining ½ cup sugar, remaining 3 tablespoons margarine, breadcrumbs, and cinnamon in a bowl; stir well. Sprinkle over apples and dough. Bake at 350° for 35 minutes or until lightly browned. Cut between apple slices into 4 lengthwise rows and 8 crosswise rows. Yield: 32 bars.

PER BAR: 92 CALORIES (22% FROM FAT)
FAT 2.2G (SATURATED FAT 0.5G)
PROTEIN 1.6G CARBOHYDRATE 16.8G
CHOLESTEROL 7MG SODIUM 47MG

SPIRAL ALMOND CHALLAH

(pictured on page 50)

This traditional Jewish yeast bread can be shaped many ways but is most commonly braided. This loaf resembles a turban after the coiled dough is baked.

3½ cups bread flour, divided
¼ teaspoon salt
1 package active dry yeast
2 tablespoons sugar
1 cup skim milk
2 tablespoons vegetable oil
2 tablespoons honey
1 egg
2 teaspoons almond extract
1½ tablespoons bread flour
Vegetable cooking spray
2 tablespoons honey
2 teaspoons skim milk
¼ cup sliced almonds, toasted

Combine 1 cup flour and next 3 ingredients in a large mixing bowl; stir well, and set aside. Combine 1 cup milk, oil, and 2 tablespoons honey in a saucepan; cook over medium heat until very warm (120° to 130°).

Gradually add liquid mixture to flour mixture, beating well at low speed of an electric mixer. Beat 2 additional minutes at medium speed. Add egg and extract, beating well. Gradually stir in enough of remaining 2½ cups flour to make a soft dough.

Sprinkle 1½ tablespoons flour evenly over work surface. Turn dough out onto floured surface, and knead until smooth and elastic (about 10 minutes). Place dough in a large bowl coated with cooking spray, turning to coat top. Cover and let rise in a warm place (85°), free from drafts, 1 hour or until doubled in bulk.

Punch dough down; turn out onto work surface, and knead lightly 4 or 5 times. Roll dough into a 32-inch rope. Form rope into a coil on a baking sheet coated with cooking spray.

Cover and let rise in a warm place, free from drafts, 20 to 25 minutes or until doubled in bulk. Bake at 350° for 25 minutes.

Combine 2 tablespoons honey and 2 teaspoons milk, stirring well. Remove loaf from oven. Brush half of honey mixture over loaf. Add almonds to remaining honey mixture; toss gently. Arrange almonds over loaf.

Return loaf to oven, and bake 5 to 8 additional minutes or until loaf sounds hollow when tapped. Remove bread from baking sheet immediately, and let cool on a wire rack. Cut into wedges to serve. Yield: 20 wedges.

PER WEDGE: 136 CALORIES (18% FROM FAT)
FAT 2.7G (SATURATED FAT 0.5G)
PROTEIN 4.1G CARBOHYDRATE 23.6G
CHOLESTEROL 11MG SODIUM 40MG

Carbonnades à la Flamande (recipe on page 72)

ENTRÉES AROUND THE WORLD

*Y*ou can learn much about a culture by looking at its mealtime entrées. For example, in a land where cooking fuel and food were once in short supply, the quick, efficient Oriental stir-fry was born. And in Spain, a country nearly surrounded by water, seafood-laden paella is popular.

The hearty main dishes featured in the following pages will introduce you to a variety of cuisines and cultures—Chinese, French, Greek, Indian, and more. First you'll find those made with beef, veal, and other meats. Several chicken recipes appear on pages 79 through 83, followed by fish and shellfish recipes.

Braciola with Noodles

BRACIOLA WITH NOODLES

Braciola *is the Italian term for a thin, rolled, stuffed piece of meat that is braised in stock or wine.*

½ cup soft breadcrumbs
½ cup minced fresh parsley
⅓ cup freshly grated Parmesan cheese
3 tablespoons capers
2 tablespoons pine nuts, toasted
2 tablespoons fresh lemon juice
1 teaspoon olive oil
4 cloves garlic, minced
1 (1½-pound) lean flank steak
Vegetable cooking spray
1½ cups low-fat spaghetti sauce
½ cup dry red wine
8 cups cooked fettuccine (about 16 ounces uncooked), cooked without salt or fat

Combine first 8 ingredients in a bowl; stir well, and set aside.

Trim fat from steak. Using a sharp knife, cut horizontally through center of steak, cutting to, but not through, other side; open flat as you would a book. Place steak between 2 sheets of heavy-duty plastic wrap, and flatten to an even thickness, using a meat mallet or rolling pin. Spread breadcrumb mixture over steak, leaving a ½-inch margin around outside edges. Roll up steak, jellyroll fashion, starting with short side. Secure at 2-inch intervals with heavy string.

Coat a large Dutch oven with cooking spray, and place over medium-high heat until hot. Add steak, and cook until browned on all sides. Remove steak from pan; set aside, and keep warm.

Add spaghetti sauce and wine to pan, scraping bottom of pan with a wooden spoon to loosen browned bits. Bring to a boil, and return steak to pan. Cover, reduce heat, and simmer 1 hour or until steak is tender. Place steak on a platter, reserving liquid. Remove string, and cut steak into 16 slices.

Spoon 1 cup pasta onto each of 8 individual plates; top with 2 steak slices and ⅓ cup sauce. Yield: 8 servings.

PER SERVING: 410 CALORIES (31% FROM FAT)
FAT 14.2G (SATURATED FAT 5.2G)
PROTEIN 24.9G CARBOHYDRATE 44.0G
CHOLESTEROL 46MG   SODIUM 531MG

The Slice Is Right

Braciola with Noodles calls for you to butter-fly the flank steak. It's not difficult once you get the hang of it, but you need to use a very sharp knife. Cut horizontally through center of steak, cutting to, but not through, other side; open flat as you would a book.

STEAK AND PEPPER STIR-FRY

Although stir-fries are typically prepared in an Oriental wok, a large nonstick skillet or sauté pan works just as well.

1 pound lean flank steak
¼ cup low-sodium soy sauce
1 tablespoon cornstarch
1 tablespoon dry sherry
1 teaspoon sugar
2 tablespoons dark sesame oil, divided
1 cup julienne-sliced green pepper
1 cup julienne-sliced sweet red pepper
1 cup vertically sliced onion
¼ teaspoon salt
¼ teaspoon dried crushed red pepper
1 tablespoon peeled, grated gingerroot
¼ cup water
6 cups cooked lo mein noodles (about 16
      ounces uncooked), cooked without salt
      or fat

Trim fat from steak. Cut steak diagonally with grain into 2-inch-thick slices. Cut slices diagonally across grain into thin strips. Combine steak, soy sauce, cornstarch, sherry, and sugar in a bowl; stir until well blended. Cover and marinate in refrigerator 15 minutes.

Heat 1 tablespoon oil in a wok or large nonstick skillet over high heat. Add green pepper and next 4 ingredients; stir-fry 1 minute. Remove pepper mixture from pan; set aside. Add remaining 1 tablespoon oil, steak mixture, and gingerroot to pan; stir-fry 2 minutes. Return pepper mixture to pan, and stir in water; stir-fry 1 minute. For each serving, spoon 1 cup steak mixture over 1 cup lo mein noodles. Yield: 6 servings.

PER SERVING: 394 CALORIES (29% FROM FAT)
FAT 12.8G (SATURATED FAT 3.9G)
PROTEIN 22.2G CARBOHYDRATE 45.3G
CHOLESTEROL 38MG   SODIUM 416MG

CARBONNADES À LA FLAMANDE

(pictured on page 68)

In this hearty French dish, beef and onions are braised in beer.

1 (1½-pound) rump roast
2 medium onions, peeled and cut into ½-inch slices
¼ teaspoon salt
¼ teaspoon pepper
3 cloves garlic, crushed
1 (13¾-ounce) can no-salt-added beef broth
1 (12-ounce) bottle beer
1½ tablespoons brown sugar
⅛ teaspoon dried thyme
1 bay leaf
12 small unpeeled round red potatoes, halved
1 tablespoon chopped fresh parsley
2 tablespoons cornstarch
⅛ teaspoon salt
1 tablespoon red wine vinegar

Trim fat from beef; cut beef into 2- x 1- x ½-inch pieces. Place a large nonstick skillet over medium-high heat until hot. Add beef, and cook until browned on all sides. Remove from pan; set aside.

Add onion to skillet. Cook over medium heat 10 minutes or until lightly browned, stirring frequently. Remove from heat; add ¼ teaspoon salt, pepper, and garlic. Stir well.

Arrange half of beef in bottom of a 3-quart casserole. Top with half of onion mixture. Repeat procedure with remaining beef and onion mixture.

Combine beef broth and next 4 ingredients; pour over onion mixture. Cover and bake at 400° for 1½ hours or until beef is tender. Set aside.

Arrange potato in a steamer basket over boiling water. Cover and steam 20 minutes or until tender; drain. Place potato in a bowl; add parsley, and toss well. Set aside; keep warm.

Strain cooking liquid from beef mixture into a saucepan, and set beef mixture aside; discard bay leaf. Combine cornstarch, ⅛ teaspoon salt, and vinegar; stir well. Add to cooking liquid. Bring to a boil, and cook, stirring constantly, 2 minutes or

until thickened. Arrange beef mixture and potato on a platter; serve with sauce. Yield: 6 servings.

PER SERVING: 261 CALORIES (16% FROM FAT)
FAT 4.7G (SATURATED FAT 1.7G)
PROTEIN 28.5G   CARBOHYDRATE 24.3G
CHOLESTEROL 65MG   SODIUM 218MG

OSSO BUCO

This Italian dish made of veal shanks is traditionally served with risotto.

2 tablespoons all-purpose flour
½ teaspoon pepper
¼ teaspoon salt
4 (10-ounce) veal shanks (1½ inches thick)
1 tablespoon olive oil
1 cup minced carrot
1 cup minced celery
1 cup minced onion
1 cup dry white wine
1 large clove garlic, minced
1 (14½-ounce) can plum tomatoes, undrained and chopped
½ cup canned beef broth, undiluted
2 teaspoons chopped fresh rosemary
1 bay leaf
Fresh rosemary sprigs (optional)

Combine first 3 ingredients in a shallow dish; stir well. Dredge veal in flour mixture.

Heat oil in a large ovenproof Dutch oven over medium-high heat. Add veal, and cook 2½ minutes on each side or until browned. Remove from pan; set aside. Reduce heat to medium; add carrot and next 4 ingredients, and cook 5 minutes, stirring frequently to deglaze pan (to loosen browned bits of food from bottom of pan).

Return veal to pan; add tomatoes and next 3 ingredients. Cover; bake at 350° for 2 hours or until veal is tender. Discard bay leaf. Serve sauce with veal. Garnish with rosemary, if desired. Yield: 4 servings.

PER SERVING: 468 CALORIES (26% FROM FAT)
FAT 13.3G (SATURATED FAT 3.4G)
PROTEIN 60.6G   CARBOHYDRATE 15.0G
CHOLESTEROL 233MG   SODIUM 742MG

Osso Buco

Dredge veal shanks in flour, pepper, and salt.

Cook veal on each side until browned; remove from pan.

Add carrot, celery, onion, wine, and garlic to pan, stirring to deglaze pan.

Moroccan Lamb Chops

MOROCCAN LAMB CHOPS

1 teaspoon ground cumin
1 teaspoon Hungarian sweet paprika
1 teaspoon ground coriander
½ teaspoon salt
¼ teaspoon ground cloves
¼ teaspoon ground red pepper
2 (1½-pound) French-cut lean racks of lamb, 8 ribs each
Vegetable cooking spray
6 cups cooked couscous (cooked without salt or fat)
1 tablespoon currants (optional)

Combine cumin and next 5 ingredients; stir well. Rub lamb with spice mixture; let stand 5 minutes.

Place lamb on rack of a broiler pan coated with cooking spray. Bake at 425° for 25 minutes or until desired degree of doneness. Let lamb stand 10 minutes before slicing. Combine couscous and currants, if desired. For each serving, top ¾ cup couscous with 2 rib chops. Yield: 8 servings.

PER SERVING: 279 CALORIES (25% FROM FAT)
FAT 7.9G (SATURATED FAT 2.7G)
PROTEIN 21.1G   CARBOHYDRATE 30.4G
CHOLESTEROL 52MG   SODIUM 200MG

MOUSSAKA

2 (1-pound) unpeeled eggplants, cut crosswise
   into ¼-inch slices
Vegetable cooking spray
2 cups skim milk
1 (¼-inch-thick) slice onion
1 bay leaf
1⅓ cups chopped onion
1 pound lean ground lamb
½ teaspoon salt, divided
1 teaspoon pumpkin pie spice
¼ teaspoon dried crushed red pepper
⅛ teaspoon pepper
1 (14½-ounce) can no-salt-added whole
   tomatoes, drained and chopped
1 tablespoon margarine
3 tablespoons all-purpose flour
1 tablespoon grated Parmesan cheese

Arrange half of eggplant slices in a single layer on a baking sheet coated with cooking spray. Broil 3 inches from heat (with electric oven door partially opened) 5 minutes on each side or until lightly browned. Repeat procedure; set aside.

Combine milk, onion slice, and bay leaf in a heavy saucepan; cook over medium heat to 180° or until tiny bubbles form around edges of pan. Discard onion and bay leaf; set scalded milk aside.

Coat a nonstick skillet with cooking spray; place over medium heat until hot. Add chopped onion; sauté 5 minutes. Add lamb, ¼ teaspoon salt, and next 3 ingredients; cook 8 minutes or until lamb is browned, stirring until meat crumbles. Drain; wipe pan drippings from skillet with a paper towel. Return meat mixture to skillet, and add tomatoes. Cook over medium heat 5 minutes or until most of liquid evaporates; set aside.

Melt margarine in a medium saucepan over medium-low heat; add flour. Cook 1 minute, stirring constantly with a wire whisk. Gradually add scalded milk and remaining ¼ teaspoon salt; cook mixture, stirring constantly, 5 minutes or until slightly thickened. Remove from heat; set aside.

Arrange half of eggplant in bottom of a 13- x 9- x 2-inch baking dish coated with cooking spray; top with half of meat mixture. Repeat procedure with remaining eggplant and meat mixture. Pour sauce over meat mixture, and sprinkle with cheese. Bake, uncovered, at 350° for 45 minutes. Yield: 6 servings.

PER SERVING: 253 CALORIES (30% FROM FAT)
FAT 8.4G (SATURATED FAT 2.7G)
PROTEIN 23.0G CARBOHYDRATE 22.2G
CHOLESTEROL 56MG SODIUM 337MG

GREEK GYROS

6 ounces lamb leg cutlets (½ inch thick), cut
   into strips
¼ cup red wine vinegar
2 tablespoons chopped fresh parsley
1 tablespoon minced onion
1 teaspoon minced garlic
½ teaspoon dried oregano
⅛ teaspoon salt
⅛ teaspoon pepper
¼ cup plain nonfat yogurt
3 tablespoons peeled, grated cucumber, drained
½ teaspoon minced garlic
⅛ teaspoon dried dillweed
Vegetable cooking spray
2 green leaf lettuce leaves
2 (8-inch) pita bread rounds, unsliced
¼ cup seeded, chopped tomato
1 tablespoon chopped green onions

Place lamb strips in a heavy-duty, zip-top plastic bag. Combine vinegar and next 6 ingredients, stirring well. Pour vinegar mixture over lamb; seal and shake until coated. Marinate in refrigerator 8 hours.

Combine yogurt and next 3 ingredients. Cover and chill. Remove lamb from bag; discard marinade. Coat a nonstick skillet with cooking spray; place over medium-high heat until hot. Add lamb; cook 2 to 3 minutes or until browned, stirring frequently. Drain and pat dry with paper towels.

Place 1 lettuce leaf on each pita round. Top each with equal amounts of lamb, tomato, yogurt mixture, and green onions. Roll up. Yield: 2 servings.

PER SERVING: 377 CALORIES (17% FROM FAT)
FAT 7.0G (SATURATED FAT 1.8G)
PROTEIN 24.1G CARBOHYDRATE 48.9G
CHOLESTEROL 55MG SODIUM 357MG

CURRIED PORK TENDERLOIN

Curry powder is a blend of several spices. Among them are cumin, ginger, coriander, chiles, and turmeric (the source of the yellow color).

1 pound pork tenderloin
1 tablespoon brown sugar
2 teaspoons curry powder
1 teaspoon dry mustard
½ teaspoon salt
½ teaspoon Hungarian sweet paprika
½ teaspoon pepper
Vegetable cooking spray
½ cup commercial mango chutney

Trim fat from pork. Combine sugar and next 5 ingredients in a small bowl; stir well. Rub pork with spice mixture.

Place pork on rack of a broiler pan coated with cooking spray; insert a meat thermometer into thickest portion of tenderloin. Bake at 425° for 25 minutes or until thermometer registers 160° (slightly pink). Let stand 5 minutes before slicing. Top each serving with 2 tablespoons chutney. Yield: 4 servings.

PER SERVING: 240 CALORIES (17% FROM FAT)
FAT 4.6G (SATURATED FAT 1.4G)
PROTEIN 25.2G CARBOHYDRATE 24.2G
CHOLESTEROL 79MG SODIUM 420MG

FYI

Chutney, from the East Indian word "chatni," is a spicy condiment containing fruit (and sometimes vegetables), vinegar, sugar, and spices. The textures range from chunky to smooth, and it is a delicious accompaniment to Indian curry dishes.

There are recipes for making your own chutney, but commercial brands are widely available.

SWEET-AND-SOUR PORK

Chinese in origin, sweet-and-sour dishes combine some form of sugar with vinegar to achieve the characteristic flavor.

¼ cup unsweetened pineapple juice
1 tablespoon cornstarch
2 tablespoons brown sugar
2 tablespoons chopped fresh cilantro
2 tablespoons white vinegar
1 tablespoon low-sodium soy sauce
¼ teaspoon dried crushed red pepper
½ pound lean boneless pork loin
¼ teaspoon garlic powder
Vegetable cooking spray
½ teaspoon vegetable oil
¼ cup chopped onion
1 cup sweet red pepper strips
½ cup coarsely chopped green pepper
½ cup sliced zucchini
1 cup coarsely chopped fresh pineapple
1 cup cooked rice (cooked without salt or fat)

Combine first 7 ingredients in a small bowl; stir well, and set aside.

Trim fat from pork; cut into 1-inch pieces. Sprinkle garlic powder over pork. Coat a wok or large nonstick skillet with cooking spray; add oil, and place over medium-high heat until hot. Add pork; cook 3 minutes or until pork loses its pink color. Add onion; stir-fry 1 minute. Add sweet red and green peppers and zucchini; stir-fry 3 minutes or until crisp-tender. Stir in pineapple juice mixture and fresh pineapple; cook, stirring constantly, 30 seconds or until thickened. Serve over rice. Yield: 2 servings.

PER SERVING: 450 CALORIES (22% FROM FAT)
FAT 11.0G (SATURATED FAT 3.3G)
PROTEIN 27.8G CARBOHYDRATE 60.6G
CHOLESTEROL 68MG SODIUM 327MG

GERMAN MEATBALLS

½ pound lean ground pork
½ pound ground round
¼ cup dry breadcrumbs
1½ tablespoons chopped fresh parsley
¼ teaspoon salt
1 teaspoon prepared mustard
½ teaspoon Worcestershire sauce
1 egg white, lightly beaten
Vegetable cooking spray
2 cloves garlic, minced
1 cup Riesling or other slightly sweet white
　wine
½ cup nonfat sour cream (at room temperature)
¼ teaspoon pepper
Cooked egg noodles (optional)

Combine first 8 ingredients; stir and shape into 24 (1-inch) meatballs. Coat a large nonstick skillet with cooking spray; place over medium heat until hot. Add meatballs; cook 10 minutes or until browned, stirring frequently. Remove from skillet; set aside.

Add garlic to skillet; sauté 30 seconds. Add wine; bring to a boil over medium heat, and cook 1 minute. Return meatballs to skillet; cover and cook 5 minutes. Remove from heat. Remove meatballs from skillet with a slotted spoon; set aside, and keep warm. Add sour cream and pepper to wine mixture in skillet; stir well. Serve meatballs and sauce over noodles, if desired. Yield: 4 servings.

PER SERVING: 224 CALORIES (27% FROM FAT)
FAT 6.8G (SATURATED FAT 2.3G)
PROTEIN 29.4G   CARBOHYDRATE 8.4G
CHOLESTEROL 68MG   SODIUM 321MG

German Meatballs

Roasted Chicken Provençal

ROASTED CHICKEN PROVENÇAL

¾ cup coarsely chopped sweet red pepper
½ cup slivered fennel bulb
2 tablespoons chopped ripe olives
2 teaspoons chopped fresh rosemary
1½ teaspoons olive oil
12 small unpeeled round red potatoes, quartered
3 large shallots, peeled and halved lengthwise
2 cloves garlic, crushed
2 teaspoons minced fresh sage
½ teaspoon coarsely ground pepper
¼ teaspoon salt
¼ teaspoon paprika
2 (4-ounce) skinned, boned chicken breast halves
Vegetable cooking spray
1½ teaspoons olive oil
⅔ cup canned low-sodium chicken broth
Fresh rosemary sprigs (optional)

Combine first 8 ingredients; toss and set aside.
Combine sage and next 3 ingredients; rub over both sides of chicken.

Coat a large ovenproof skillet with cooking spray. Add 1½ teaspoons oil; place over medium-high heat until hot. Add chicken; cook 1 minute on each side or until browned. Remove from skillet, and set aside.

Remove skillet from heat. Add vegetable mixture to skillet; stir. Return chicken to skillet, nestling it into vegetables; bake, uncovered, at 450° for 20 minutes. Remove chicken from skillet; stir vegetables, scraping bottom of skillet to loosen browned bits. Return chicken to skillet. Reduce temperature to 375°; bake 15 additional minutes.

Place 1 chicken breast half and 1⅓ cups vegetable mixture on each of 2 serving plates. Add chicken broth to skillet; bring to a boil over high heat, and cook 1 minute, scraping bottom of skillet to loosen browned bits. Spoon 3 tablespoons sauce over each serving. Garnish with rosemary, if desired. Yield: 2 servings.

PER SERVING: 403 CALORIES (24% FROM FAT)
FAT 10.6G (SATURATED FAT 1.6G)
PROTEIN 33.6G   CARBOHYDRATE 45.0G
CHOLESTEROL 66MG   SODIUM 490MG

CAJUN CHICKEN MAQUE CHOUX

Maque choux *is a Cajun term for corn that has been fried and then simmered.*

2 teaspoons garlic powder
1 teaspoon onion powder
1 teaspoon dried oregano
1 teaspoon dried thyme
1 tablespoon plus 1 teaspoon paprika
1 teaspoon ground red pepper
½ teaspoon salt
4 (4-ounce) skinned, boned chicken breast halves
2 slices bacon
2 cups chopped sweet red pepper
2 cups chopped onion
4 cups fresh corn cut from cob (about 5 large ears)
1 cup diced tomato
1 cup evaporated skimmed milk
¼ teaspoon salt
½ cup chopped fresh parsley

Combine garlic powder and next 6 ingredients; stir well. Place 2 tablespoons herb mixture in a shallow dish, and dredge chicken in herb mixture; set aside.

Cook bacon in a large Dutch oven over medium-high heat until crisp. Remove from pan; set aside.

Add chicken to pan, and cook over medium-high heat 1 minute on each side or until browned. Remove from pan, and set aside. Add sweet red pepper and onion to pan, and sauté 5 minutes. Add corn, remaining herb mixture, tomato, milk, and ¼ teaspoon salt; cook over medium heat 30 minutes. Add chicken to corn mixture in pan; cook 15 minutes or until chicken is done.

Spoon 1¼ cups corn mixture onto each of 4 individual plates, and top with 1 chicken breast half. Crumble bacon over each serving, and sprinkle with parsley. Yield: 4 servings.

PER SERVING: 471 CALORIES (17% FROM FAT)
FAT 8.9G (SATURATED FAT 2.3G)
PROTEIN 49.1G   CARBOHYDRATE 53.9G
CHOLESTEROL 102MG   SODIUM 696MG

GRILLED JERK CHICKEN

When Jamaicans barbecue, they call it jerk. This style of outdoor cooking is best known for its hot habañero chiles and its wood smoke flavor.

Hickory chips
Wet Jerk Rub
6 (4-ounce) skinned, boned chicken breast
   halves
Vegetable cooking spray
4 cups cooked long-grain rice (cooked without
   salt or fat)
3 tablespoons fresh lime juice
2 tablespoons peeled, grated gingerroot
½ teaspoon freshly grated nutmeg
¼ teaspoon salt

Soak hickory chips in water at least 30 minutes, and drain.

Set aside ½ cup Wet Jerk Rub. Coat chicken with remaining 1 cup Wet Jerk Rub. Place chicken in a large heavy-duty, zip-top plastic bag; seal bag, and marinate in refrigerator 8 hours.

Rubbing It In

Jerk is the term for a style of barbecue that includes marinating the meat in a green pesto-like mixture of herbs, spices, and the hottest peppers in the world. A little oil and lime juice make it a sauce-like "wet rub."

Preheat gas grill to medium-hot (350° to 400°) using both burners. After preheating, turn left burner off. Place hickory chips in a disposable aluminum foil pan or an aluminum foil packet poked with holes on grill over right burner. Coat grill rack with cooking spray, and place on grill over medium-hot coals. Place chicken on rack over left burner. Grill, covered, 30 minutes or until done, turning frequently. Transfer chicken to a platter, and keep warm.

Combine cooked rice and remaining 4 ingredients; toss gently. Spoon rice mixture evenly onto individual serving plates. Top rice with chicken. Serve immediately with reserved Wet Jerk Rub. Yield: 6 servings.

WET JERK RUB

4 cups coarsely chopped green onions
¼ cup fresh thyme leaves
3 tablespoons peeled, grated gingerroot
1 tablespoon freshly ground pepper
1 tablespoon freshly ground coriander seeds
2 tablespoons vegetable oil
2 tablespoons fresh lime juice
2 teaspoons salt
2 teaspoons freshly ground allspice
1 teaspoon freshly ground nutmeg
1 teaspoon ground cinnamon
5 cloves garlic, peeled and halved
3 bay leaves
1 to 2 habañero chile peppers, halved and
   seeded

Position knife blade in food processor bowl; add all ingredients, and process until smooth, scraping sides of bowl once. Use 1 to 2 tablespoons to rub or brush onto chicken pieces or fish before grilling. Yield: 1½ cups.

Note: For the most flavor, use freshly ground spices. You can grind whole allspice and nutmeg in a coffee grinder. Or you can use a nutmeg grater (available in most kitchen shops).

PER SERVING: 375 CALORIES (21% FROM FAT)
FAT 8.6G (SATURATED FAT 1.9G)
PROTEIN 31.0G   CARBOHYDRATE 43.4G
CHOLESTEROL 72MG   SODIUM 955MG

Chicken in Citrus Sauce

CHICKEN IN CITRUS SAUCE

½ cup water
2 tablespoons (½-inch) julienne-sliced orange rind
1 tablespoon (½-inch) julienne-sliced grapefruit rind
2 teaspoons (½-inch) julienne-sliced lemon rind
1 teaspoon (½-inch) julienne-sliced lime rind
¾ cup fresh orange juice
2 tablespoons fresh grapefruit juice
2 teaspoons fresh lemon juice
2 teaspoons fresh lime juice
¾ cup canned low-salt chicken broth, undiluted
¼ cup dry red wine
1 teaspoon sugar
¼ teaspoon salt
¼ teaspoon pepper
8 chicken thighs (about 3 pounds), skinned
1 teaspoon margarine
1 tablespoon white wine vinegar
½ teaspoon cornstarch

Combine first 5 ingredients in a small saucepan; bring to a boil. Cover, reduce heat, and simmer 10 minutes. Drain, reserving citrus rind. Combine citrus rind, citrus juices, broth, wine, and sugar in a small bowl; stir well, and set aside.

Sprinkle salt and pepper over chicken. Melt margarine in a large nonstick skillet over medium-high heat. Add chicken; cook 3 minutes on each side. Add juice mixture; cover, reduce heat, and simmer 35 minutes. Remove chicken from skillet with tongs or a slotted spoon; set aside, and keep warm.

Combine vinegar and cornstarch; stir well. Add cornstarch mixture to juice mixture in skillet; simmer, stirring constantly, 10 minutes or until mixture is thickened and slightly reduced. To serve, spoon sauce over chicken. Yield: 4 servings.

PER SERVING: 198 CALORIES (29% FROM FAT)
FAT 6.3G (SATURATED FAT 1.5G)
PROTEIN 26.0G   CARBOHYDRATE 9.8G
CHOLESTEROL 106MG   SODIUM 284MG

Mexican Chicken Mole

Mexican Chicken Mole

¾ cup chopped green pepper
½ cup chopped onion
1 tablespoon vegetable oil
1 clove garlic, minced
1 tablespoon sugar
3 tablespoons unsweetened cocoa
1 tablespoon chili powder
1 teaspoon ground cumin
½ teaspoon salt
1 (14.5-ounce) can no-salt-added whole
    tomatoes, undrained and chopped
1 (4.5-ounce) can chopped green chiles,
    drained
3 (4-ounce) skinned, boned chicken thighs
3 (4-ounce) skinned, boned chicken breast
    halves
¼ teaspoon salt
1 tablespoon water
2 teaspoons cornstarch
6 cups cooked long-grain rice (cooked without
    salt or fat)
Cilantro sprigs (optional)

Combine first 4 ingredients in a 2-quart casserole. Cover with heavy-duty plastic wrap, and vent. Microwave at HIGH 4 minutes or until tender. Add sugar and next 6 ingredients; stir well. Arrange chicken over tomato mixture, and sprinkle with ¼ teaspoon salt. Cover and microwave at HIGH 8 minutes. Rearrange chicken, spooning tomato mixture over chicken; cover and microwave at HIGH 8 minutes or until chicken is done. Remove chicken from dish; set aside, and keep warm.

Combine water and cornstarch, stirring until blended; add to tomato mixture. Microwave, uncovered, at HIGH 5 minutes, stirring after 2½ minutes. To serve, spoon 1 cup rice onto each individual serving plate; top with 1 piece chicken and ½ cup tomato mixture. Garnish with cilantro sprigs, if desired. Yield: 6 servings.

PER SERVING: 409 CALORIES (15% FROM FAT)
FAT 6.7G (SATURATED FAT 1.6G)
PROTEIN 30.5G CARBOHYDRATE 54.8G
CHOLESTEROL 78MG SODIUM 428MG

Tandoori Chicken and Couscous

The traditional tandoor, a round-topped oven used throughout India and in Indian restaurants, is made of clay and brick. Here the microwave replaces its high-heat method (usually over 500°F), but the flavors are typical of tandoori dishes.

3 skinned chicken breast halves (about 1½
    pounds)
3 skinned chicken thighs (about ¾ pound)
3 skinned chicken drumsticks (about ½
    pound)
½ teaspoon salt, divided
½ teaspoon black pepper, divided
1 cup plain nonfat yogurt
1½ tablespoons fresh lime juice
1½ teaspoons ground coriander
1 teaspoon ground turmeric
2 teaspoons peeled, grated gingerroot
¼ teaspoon ground red pepper
2 cloves garlic, minced
½ teaspoon paprika
6 cups cooked couscous (cooked without salt
    or fat)

Place chicken in a 10- x 10-inch casserole, and sprinkle with ¼ teaspoon salt and ¼ teaspoon black pepper.

Combine remaining ¼ teaspoon salt and ¼ teaspoon black pepper, yogurt, and next 6 ingredients in a bowl, and stir well. Pour yogurt mixture over chicken; cover and marinate in refrigerator for at least 8 hours.

Uncover and sprinkle with paprika. Cover with wax paper, and microwave at HIGH 18 to 20 minutes, rotating dish a half-turn after 9 minutes. Let stand, covered, 10 minutes. Remove chicken from dish, and discard yogurt mixture. To serve, spoon 1 cup couscous onto each of 6 individual serving plates; top with 1 chicken breast half or 1 chicken thigh and 1 drumstick. Yield: 6 servings.

PER SERVING: 390 CALORIES (17% FROM FAT)
FAT 7.4G (SATURATED FAT 1.9G)
PROTEIN 35.7G CARBOHYDRATE 44.3G
CHOLESTEROL 84MG SODIUM 307MG

GREEK RED SNAPPER

1 tablespoon olive oil
2 cups chopped onion
2½ cups seeded, chopped tomato
½ cup minced fresh parsley
½ cup dry white wine
⅛ teaspoon pepper
4 bay leaves
2 large cloves garlic, minced
8 (6-ounce) snapper or grouper fillets
Vegetable cooking spray
1½ tablespoons fresh lemon juice
½ teaspoon salt
4 peeled medium baking potatoes (about
    1¾ pounds), each cut lengthwise into
    12 wedges
1 tablespoon olive oil
¼ teaspoon salt
8 (½-inch-thick) slices tomato
8 (¼-inch-thick) rings green pepper

Heat 1 tablespoon oil in a large nonstick skillet over medium heat. Add onion; sauté 7 minutes or until tender. Add chopped tomato and next 5 ingredients; reduce heat, and simmer, uncovered, 15 minutes or until liquid evaporates, stirring occasionally. Set aside.

Arrange fillets in a 13- x 9- x 2-inch baking dish coated with cooking spray. Sprinkle lemon juice and ½ teaspoon salt over fillets, and top with onion mixture. Place potato wedges over onion mixture, and drizzle with 1 tablespoon oil and ¼ teaspoon salt. Top with tomato slices and pepper rings. Bake, uncovered, at 350° for 1 hour and 20 minutes or until potato is tender.

Place 1 fillet and 6 potato wedges on each of 8 individual serving plates. Divide onion mixture evenly among servings, and top each serving with 1 tomato slice and 1 pepper ring. Yield: 8 servings.

PER SERVING: 296 CALORIES (19% FROM FAT)
FAT 6.2G (SATURATED FAT 1.0G)
PROTEIN 38.8G CARBOHYDRATE 20.8G
CHOLESTEROL 63MG SODIUM 350MG

CAJUN-BLACKENED SWORDFISH STEAKS

What's the difference between Cajun and Creole? Flavorful and robust, Cajun cooking uses many spices and often calls for a darkened roux, while Creole cookery relies on heavy doses of butter, cream, and tomatoes.

4 (4-ounce) swordfish steaks (½ inch thick)
Cajun Seasoning Blend

Dredge fish in Cajun Seasoning Blend; set aside. Place a large cast-iron skillet over medium-high heat 5 minutes or until very hot. Add fish, and cook 3 minutes. Turn fish, and cook 2 to 3 additional minutes or until fish flakes easily when tested with a fork. Fish should look charred. (You may prefer to do this procedure outside due to the small amount of smoke that is created.) Yield: 4 servings.

CAJUN SEASONING BLEND
2 teaspoons dried basil
2 teaspoons crushed black peppercorns
1 teaspoon ground white pepper
1 teaspoon cumin seeds, crushed
1 teaspoon caraway seeds, crushed
1 teaspoon fennel seeds, crushed
1 teaspoon dried thyme
1 teaspoon dried oregano
½ teaspoon salt
½ teaspoon dried crushed red pepper
2 teaspoons paprika

Combine first 10 ingredients in a small skillet; place over medium-high heat. Cook, stirring constantly, 3 minutes or until seeds are lightly browned. Remove from heat; stir in paprika. Store in an airtight container; shake well before each use. Use to coat chicken, beef, pork, or fish, or sprinkle over grilled corn or baked potatoes. Yield: ¼ cup.

PER SERVING: 155 CALORIES (30% FROM FAT)
FAT 5.1G (SATURATED FAT 1.3G)
PROTEIN 23.3G CARBOHYDRATE 3.4G
CHOLESTEROL 44MG SODIUM 399MG

MARYLAND CRAB CAKES

1 pound lump crabmeat, shell pieces removed
1⅓ cups soft breadcrumbs
⅓ cup minced green onions
⅓ cup chopped fresh parsley
2 tablespoons lemon juice
1 tablespoon 2% low-fat milk
1 teaspoon hot sauce
½ teaspoon salt
¼ teaspoon pepper
4 egg whites
1⅓ cups soft breadcrumbs
2 tablespoons vegetable oil, divided
Lemon wedges (optional)

Combine first 10 ingredients in a bowl; stir well. Divide crabmeat mixture into 8 equal portions.

Place 1⅓ cups breadcrumbs in a shallow dish. Dredge crabmeat portions in breadcrumbs, shaping into patties about 3½ inches wide and ½ inch thick.

Heat 1 tablespoon oil in a large nonstick skillet over medium-high heat. Add 4 patties, and cook 3 minutes. Carefully turn patties, and cook 3 minutes or until golden. Repeat procedure with remaining 1 tablespoon oil and patties. Serve with lemon wedges, if desired. Yield: 8 servings.

PER SERVING: 189 CALORIES (26% FROM FAT)
FAT 5.5G (SATURATED FAT 1.0G)
PROTEIN 16.2G CARBOHYDRATE 17.8G
CHOLESTEROL 58MG SODIUM 506MG

Maryland Crab Cakes

MOULES MARINIÈRE

Moules means "mussels" in French, while marinière refers to a sauce made with onions, white wine, and herbs.

2 cups dry white wine
1 cup finely chopped onion
⅓ cup chopped fresh flat-leaf parsley
½ teaspoon salt
½ teaspoon freshly ground pepper
4 thyme sprigs
3 cloves garlic, minced
2 bay leaves
5 pounds fresh mussels, scrubbed and
    debearded (about 100 mussels)
1½ tablespoons all-purpose flour
1½ tablespoons margarine, softened
5 (1-ounce) slices French bread

Combine first 8 ingredients in a large stockpot; stir well. Add mussels; cover and cook over high heat 13 minutes or until mussels open, stirring well after 3 minutes. Discard thyme, bay leaves, and any unopened shells. Remove mussels with a slotted spoon, and divide into 5 individual shallow bowls.

Combine flour and margarine in a small bowl; stir well. Add flour mixture to wine mixture, stirring with a wire whisk until blended. Bring to a boil, and cook 8 minutes or until slightly thickened. Spoon ¾ cup wine mixture over mussels in each bowl. Serve with French bread. Yield: 5 servings.

PER SERVING: 200 CALORIES (24% FROM FAT)
FAT 5.3G (SATURATED FAT 1.0G)
PROTEIN 12.1G CARBOHYDRATE 25.5G
CHOLESTEROL 20MG SODIUM 654MG

COQUILLES ST. JACQUES À LA PROVENÇAL

This famous scallop dish is so named because the French word for both the main ingredient and the shape of the baking dish is coquille.

1½ tablespoons margarine, divided
⅓ cup minced onion
2 tablespoons minced shallots
1 clove garlic, minced
½ cup all-purpose flour
1¼ pounds fresh sea scallops
⅔ cup dry white wine
⅛ teaspoon salt
⅛ teaspoon dried thyme
1 small bay leaf
Dash of ground white pepper
¼ cup plus 2 tablespoons (1½ ounces)
    shredded Swiss cheese

Melt 1½ teaspoons margarine in a nonstick skillet over medium heat; add onion. Sauté 3 minutes or until lightly browned. Add shallots and garlic, and sauté 1 minute. Remove onion mixture from skillet, and set aside.

Place flour in a zip-top plastic bag; add scallops. Toss bag to coat scallops. Melt remaining 1 tablespoon margarine in a skillet over medium heat. Remove scallops from bag, shaking off excess flour. Add scallops to skillet; sauté 4 minutes or until golden.

Return onion mixture to skillet; add wine and next 4 ingredients. Cover, reduce heat, and simmer 4 minutes. Uncover and bring to a boil; cook 1 minute. Discard bay leaf. Divide scallop mixture evenly among 6 individual gratin dishes. Top each with 1 tablespoon cheese. Broil 5½ inches from heat (with electric oven door partially opened) 30 seconds or until cheese melts. Serve immediately. Yield: 6 servings.

Note: Substitute ⅔ cup canned low-sodium chicken broth for dry white wine, if desired.

PER SERVING: 180 CALORIES (28% FROM FAT)
FAT 5.6G (SATURATED FAT 1.9G)
PROTEIN 19.2G CARBOHYDRATE 12.2G
CHOLESTEROL 38MG · SODIUM 256MG

Shrimp Jambalaya

SHRIMP JAMBALAYA

½ pound unpeeled medium-size fresh shrimp
Vegetable cooking spray
1 tablespoon vegetable oil
1 tablespoon all-purpose flour
1 cup chopped onion
1 cup chopped celery
1 cup chopped green pepper
2 cloves garlic, minced
¼ pound reduced-fat, low-salt ham, diced
2½ cups canned no-salt-added chicken broth
1 (14½-ounce) can no-salt-added whole
    tomatoes, undrained and chopped
¼ cup chopped fresh parsley
1 teaspoon dried thyme
½ teaspoon salt
½ teaspoon dried basil
¼ teaspoon black pepper
⅛ teaspoon ground red pepper
1 cup long-grain rice, uncooked

Peel and devein shrimp; set aside.

Coat a large nonstick skillet with cooking spray; add oil, and stir in flour. Cook over medium-high heat, stirring constantly, 1½ minutes or until browned. Add onion and next 4 ingredients; sauté 7 minutes or until tender. Add chicken broth and next 7 ingredients; bring to a boil. Stir in rice; cover, reduce heat, and simmer 20 minutes or until rice is tender. Stir in shrimp; cover and cook 5 minutes or until shrimp turn pink. Yield: 4 (1½-cup) servings.

PER SERVING: 356 CALORIES (16% FROM FAT)
FAT 6.4G (SATURATED FAT 1.4G)
PROTEIN 19.7G CARBOHYDRATE 53.1G
CHOLESTEROL 79MG SODIUM 625MG

SHRIMP ÉTOUFFÉE

A popular Cajun dish, étouffée is a thick, spicy stew that derives its flavor from a dark brown roux made by cooking flour and fat to a deep golden brown.

1½ pounds unpeeled medium-size fresh shrimp
Vegetable cooking spray
2 cups chopped onion
1 cup chopped green pepper
½ cup chopped celery
2 cloves garlic, minced
3 tablespoons margarine
3 tablespoons all-purpose flour
¼ cup water
¼ teaspoon salt
¼ teaspoon black pepper
⅛ teaspoon ground red pepper
1 (8-ounce) bottle clam juice
6 cups cooked long-grain rice (cooked without salt or fat)

Peel and devein shrimp; set aside.

Coat a large, heavy saucepan with cooking spray; place over medium-high heat until hot. Add onion and next 3 ingredients, and sauté 10 minutes or until tender. Remove from pan; set aside.

Melt margarine in pan over medium heat; stir in flour. Cook, stirring constantly, 7 minutes or until very brown. Gradually add water, blending with a wire whisk. Stir in onion mixture, salt, and next 3 ingredients; bring to a boil. Cover, reduce heat, and simmer 15 minutes. Add shrimp; cook 10 additional minutes or until shrimp turn pink. For each serving, spoon ⅔ cup shrimp mixture over 1 cup rice. Yield: 6 servings.

PER SERVING: 410 CALORIES (17% FROM FAT)
FAT 7.7G (SATURATED FAT 1.4G)
PROTEIN 23.0G CARBOHYDRATE 60.2G
CHOLESTEROL 129MG SODIUM 383MG

PAELLA

This Spanish dish is named after the wide, shallow two-handled pan in which it is prepared and served.

16 fresh mussels, scrubbed and debearded
8 small clams in shells, scrubbed
2 tablespoons cornmeal
1 pound unpeeled medium-size fresh shrimp
2 (10½-ounce) cans low-sodium chicken broth
¼ teaspoon salt
⅛ teaspoon pepper
½ teaspoon threads of saffron
Vegetable cooking spray
1 tablespoon olive oil
1 pound skinned, boned chicken breasts, cut into 1-inch pieces
1 cup chopped onion
2 small cloves garlic, minced
2 cups (2-inch) sweet red pepper strips
2 cups chopped unpeeled tomato
1½ cups Arborio rice, uncooked
½ cup water
1 cup frozen English peas, thawed

Place mussels and clams in a large bowl; cover with cold water. Sprinkle with cornmeal; let stand 30 minutes. Drain; rinse mussels and clams under running water. Set aside. Peel and devein shrimp; set aside.

Place broth, salt, and pepper in a saucepan; bring to a simmer. Add saffron, and simmer 10 minutes. (Do not boil.) Keep mixture warm over low heat.

Coat a nonstick electric skillet with cooking spray; add oil, and heat at medium (350°) until hot. Add chicken, onion, and garlic; sauté 5 minutes or until chicken is lightly browned. Add sweet red pepper and tomato; sauté 3 minutes.

Add rice, and cook, stirring constantly, 2 minutes. Reduce heat to medium-low, and add ½ cup warm broth mixture; cook 5 minutes or until liquid is nearly absorbed, stirring occasionally. Repeat procedure with remaining broth mixture, adding ½ cup broth mixture at a time.

Stir water into rice mixture; place mussels and clams, hinged side down, on top of rice mixture. Top with shrimp and peas. Cover and cook 10 minutes or until mussels and clams open and shrimp turn pink. Discard any unopened shells. Yield: 8 servings.

Paella

Note: Substitute long-grain rice for Arborio rice, if desired. Add rice to chicken mixture; cook, stirring constantly, 1 minute. Add chicken broth mixture and 1 cup water; bring to a boil. Reduce heat, and simmer, uncovered, 10 minutes. Place mussels and clams on top of rice mixture. Top with shrimp and peas. Cover and cook 10 minutes or until mussels and clams open and shrimp turn pink.

PER SERVING: 330 CALORIES (13% FROM FAT)
FAT 4.6G (SATURATED FAT 0.7G)
PROTEIN 29.3G   CARBOHYDRATE 41.3G
CHOLESTEROL 103MG   SODIUM 217MG

Pesto-Stuffed Pasta Shells (recipe on page 105)

VEGETARIAN CUISINE

*M*eals without meat are commonplace in many cultures. Among Italian favorites, Eggplant Parmesan (page 97) and Four-Cheese Manicotti (page 103) are two of the best examples of meatless main dishes. Rich with cheese and pasta, each contains more than 10 grams of protein per serving yet calories from fat are under 30 percent.

In this chapter, you'll find recipes from several regions that combine protein-rich cheese, beans, or tofu with high-carbohydrate pasta, rice, couscous, or tortillas.

Eggs (or egg substitutes) provide protein in the dishes on pages 98 and 99. Try Huevos Rancheros for an authentic Mexican breakfast. Another day enjoy West Coast Breakfast Burritos or the Greek-inspired Spanakopita Quiche.

Cajun Beans and Rice Casserole

1 (16-ounce) can red beans, drained
1 (15-ounce) can no-salt-added pinto beans, drained
1 (14½-ounce) can no-salt-added stewed tomatoes
Vegetable cooking spray
2 cups chopped onion
½ cup chopped celery
½ cup chopped green pepper
1 teaspoon dried thyme
½ teaspoon dried oregano
½ teaspoon black pepper
¼ teaspoon salt
¼ teaspoon onion powder
⅛ teaspoon ground white pepper
3 cups cooked long-grain rice (cooked without salt or fat)
1 (8-ounce) carton low-fat sour cream
½ cup (2 ounces) shredded reduced-fat Cheddar cheese

Mash red and pinto beans slightly with a fork. Combine beans and tomatoes in a medium saucepan; bring to a boil. Reduce heat; simmer, uncovered, 25 minutes or until most of liquid evaporates.

Coat a large nonstick skillet with cooking spray; place over medium-high heat until hot. Add onion, celery, and green pepper; sauté 4 minutes or until tender. Add thyme and next 5 ingredients; cook 5 minutes, stirring frequently. Stir half of onion mixture into bean mixture.

Combine remaining onion mixture, rice, and sour cream. Spoon half of rice mixture into an 11- x 7- x 1½-inch baking dish coated with cooking spray; top with half of bean mixture. Repeat layers with remaining rice and bean mixtures.

Cover and bake at 325° for 25 minutes. Uncover and sprinkle with cheese. Bake, uncovered, 5 additional minutes or until cheese melts. Let stand 5 minutes before serving. Yield: 6 servings.

PER SERVING: 354 CALORIES (18% FROM FAT)
FAT 7.2G (SATURATED FAT 4.0G)
PROTEIN 14.6G   CARBOHYDRATE 58.9G
CHOLESTEROL 20MG   SODIUM 345MG

Italian White Bean and Spinach Cups

Sun-dried tomato sprinkles can be found in the canned-tomato section of the supermarket.

2 large sweet red peppers (about 1 pound)
1 teaspoon olive oil
½ cup sliced green onions
1 clove garlic, minced
1 cup thinly sliced spinach leaves
⅓ cup canned low-salt chicken broth, undiluted
1 (19-ounce) can cannellini beans or other white beans, drained and divided
½ cup (2 ounces) crumbled feta cheese with basil and tomato
2 tablespoons sun-dried tomato sprinkles
2 tablespoons sliced ripe olives
1 tablespoon balsamic vinegar
½ teaspoon dried Italian seasoning
2 teaspoons Italian-seasoned breadcrumbs
1 teaspoon grated Parmesan cheese

Cut tops off peppers; discard tops, seeds, and membranes. Cook peppers in boiling water 5 minutes; drain and set aside.

Heat oil in a large nonstick skillet over medium-high heat. Add green onions and garlic; sauté 2 minutes. Stir in spinach; cook 1 minute or until spinach wilts. Remove from heat, and set aside.

Place broth and ½ cup beans in container of a food processor or electric blender; process until smooth. Stir bean puree into spinach mixture. Add remaining beans, feta cheese, tomato sprinkles, olives, vinegar, and Italian seasoning; stir well.

Divide bean mixture evenly between peppers. Combine breadcrumbs and Parmesan cheese; sprinkle evenly over bean mixture. Place stuffed peppers in an 8-inch square baking dish; bake at 350° for 25 minutes. Yield: 2 servings.

PER SERVING: 369 CALORIES (29% FROM FAT)
FAT 11.9G (SATURATED FAT 5.2G)
PROTEIN 18.0G   CARBOHYDRATE 49.6G
CHOLESTEROL 26MG   SODIUM 986MG

Santa Fe Stuffed Chiles

SANTA FE STUFFED CHILES

Poblano chiles are usually dark green and have a rich flavor that runs from mild to slightly hot.

3 medium poblano chiles (about 9 ounces)
⅓ cup grated Parmesan cheese
½ cup fresh corn cut from cob (about 1 ear)
½ cup finely chopped purple onion
⅓ cup finely chopped plum tomato
¼ cup fine, dry breadcrumbs
¼ cup chopped fresh cilantro
2 tablespoons plain nonfat yogurt
2 tablespoons reduced-fat mayonnaise
1 teaspoon chili powder
½ teaspoon pepper
Vegetable cooking spray
2 tablespoons plain nonfat yogurt
Fresh cilantro sprigs (optional)

Cut chiles in half lengthwise; discard seeds and membranes.

Combine cheese and next 9 ingredients in a bowl; stir well. Divide vegetable mixture evenly among chile halves. Place stuffed chiles on a baking sheet coated with cooking spray. Bake at 375° for 20 minutes. To serve, spoon 1 teaspoon yogurt onto each chile half. Garnish with cilantro sprigs, if desired. Yield: 2 servings.

PER SERVING: 310 CALORIES (30% FROM FAT)
FAT 11.2G (SATURATED FAT 5.2G)
PROTEIN 16.2G CARBOHYDRATE 39.7G
CHOLESTEROL 16MG SODIUM 705MG

Stuffed Green Chiles with Yellow Pepper Sauce

STUFFED GREEN CHILES WITH YELLOW PEPPER SAUCE

12 whole fresh green chiles (about 2 pounds)
¼ cup plus 2 tablespoons nonfat sour cream
¼ cup plus 2 tablespoons plain nonfat yogurt
¼ teaspoon salt
¼ teaspoon ground cumin
Vegetable cooking spray
2 teaspoons vegetable oil
½ cup minced green onions
2 cloves garlic, minced
1 (15-ounce) can pinto beans, drained
½ teaspoon ground oregano
½ teaspoon ground cumin
½ cup minced fresh cilantro
Yellow Pepper Sauce
1½ cups diced, seeded tomato
Fresh cilantro sprigs (optional)

Make a lengthwise slit down each chile, and carefully remove seeds. Place chiles on a baking sheet, skin side up. Broil 5½ inches from heat (with electric oven door partially opened) 15 to 20 minutes or until charred, turning occasionally. Place in ice water; chill 5 minutes. Remove from water; peel chiles, and discard skins. Set aside.

Combine sour cream and next 3 ingredients in a small bowl; stir well. Cover and chill.

Coat a large nonstick skillet with cooking spray; add oil. Place over medium-high heat until hot. Add green onions and garlic; sauté 2 minutes. Add pinto beans, oregano, and ½ teaspoon cumin; stir well. Reduce heat to low; cook until mixture is thoroughly heated, mashing beans slightly with a potato masher. Remove from heat; stir in minced cilantro.

Carefully stuff bean mixture evenly into chiles; gently reshape chiles. Arrange chiles in a single layer in a 13- x 9- x 2-inch baking dish coated with cooking spray. Bake at 325° for 15 minutes or until thoroughly heated.

Spoon ¼ cup Yellow Pepper Sauce onto each individual serving plate. Spoon sour cream mixture into a zip-top plastic bag, and seal. Snip a tiny hole in one corner of bag. Pipe mixture in thin parallel lines, ½ inch apart, across sauce. Pull point of a wooden pick back and forth perpendicular to lines to create a webbed pattern. Arrange 3 chiles over sauce on each plate; top evenly with tomato. Garnish with cilantro sprigs, if desired. Yield: 4 servings.

YELLOW PEPPER SAUCE

1 cup chopped sweet yellow pepper
⅔ cup peeled, diced potato
⅓ cup dry white wine
⅓ cup canned low-sodium chicken broth, undiluted

Combine all ingredients in a small saucepan; stir well. Bring to a boil; cover, reduce heat, and simmer 20 minutes or until pepper and potato are tender. Transfer mixture to container of an electric blender; cover and process until smooth. Strain through a sieve. Serve warm. Yield: 1 cup.

PER SERVING: 235 CALORIES (16% FROM FAT)
FAT 4.1G (SATURATED FAT 0.6G)
PROTEIN 11.2G CARBOHYDRATE 42.2G
CHOLESTEROL 0MG SODIUM 207MG

Pepper Alert!

When Christopher Columbus landed in America, he found an unusual spicy vegetable known today as the chile pepper. Now cooks around the world use more than 200 varieties of the chile to add zest to their food.

Chile peppers vary from mildly warm to blistering hot. Most of the pepper's heat is located in the seeds and membranes. In fact, the seeds and membranes can burn the skin, so it's wise to wear rubber gloves or to at least wash your hands thoroughly after handling hot chile peppers. Most importantly, don't touch your eyes or the sensitive skin on your face because the pepper juice might cause a painful burn.

CHINESE VEGETABLE STIR-FRY

Tofu is a protein-rich soybean product with a very mild flavor. It absorbs the flavors of the recipe and adds texture to the dish.

¼ cup fresh lemon juice
¼ cup low-sodium soy sauce
1 tablespoon peeled, grated gingerroot
2 teaspoons sugar
2 cloves garlic, minced
1 (10-ounce) package firm tofu, drained and cubed
1 cup chopped onion
2 tablespoons vegetable oil
2 cups shredded Chinese cabbage
1 cup fresh bean sprouts
1 cup diced sweet red pepper
1 cup sliced fresh mushrooms
¼ cup sliced green onions
2 teaspoons cornstarch
6 cups cooked brown rice (cooked without salt or fat)

Combine first 5 ingredients in a medium bowl, stirring well. Add tofu and chopped onion. Cover and marinate in refrigerator 2 to 3 hours. Drain tofu and onion, reserving marinade.

Drizzle oil around top of wok, coating sides. Heat at medium (350°) until hot. Add tofu and onion; stir-fry 10 minutes or until tofu starts to brown and onion is tender. Remove tofu mixture from wok; set aside, and keep warm.

Add cabbage and next 4 ingredients to wok, and stir-fry 2 to 3 minutes or until vegetables are crisp-tender. Combine reserved marinade and cornstarch, stirring well. Add marinade mixture to vegetables; cook, stirring constantly, 3 minutes or until thickened. Add tofu mixture, and cook 30 seconds or until thoroughly heated. To serve, spoon 1 cup rice onto each individual serving plate. Top evenly with vegetable mixture. Yield: 6 servings.

PER SERVING: 339 CALORIES (24% FROM FAT)
FAT 8.9G (SATURATED FAT 1.6G)
PROTEIN 10.6G CARBOHYDRATE 55.3G
CHOLESTEROL 0MG SODIUM 291MG

SOUTH-OF-THE-BORDER BAKE

2 cups no-salt-added tomato sauce
1 tablespoon white vinegar
1 to 1½ teaspoons chili powder
¼ teaspoon garlic powder
¼ teaspoon ground cumin
⅛ to ¼ teaspoon ground red pepper
4 cups sliced zucchini
1½ cups frozen whole kernel corn, thawed
1½ cups (6 ounces) shredded reduced-fat sharp Cheddar cheese, divided
¾ cup crushed baked tortilla chips
1 (4.5-ounce) can chopped green chiles, undrained
Vegetable cooking spray
½ cup nonfat sour cream
½ cup chopped green pepper
½ cup chopped tomato

Combine first 6 ingredients in a medium saucepan; bring to a simmer over medium heat, stirring frequently. Reduce heat to low, and cook, uncovered, 12 minutes; set aside.

Combine zucchini, corn, ¾ cup cheese, chips, and green chiles in a bowl; stir well. Spoon zucchini mixture into a 13- x 9- x 2-inch baking dish coated with cooking spray. Pour tomato sauce mixture over casserole; bake, uncovered, at 350° for 25 minutes. Sprinkle remaining ¾ cup cheese over casserole, and bake 5 additional minutes.

Spread sour cream over casserole, and sprinkle with green pepper and tomato. Yield: 8 servings.

PER SERVING: 157 CALORIES (26% FROM FAT)
FAT 4.6G (SATURATED FAT 2.4G)
PROTEIN 10.3G CARBOHYDRATE 20.8G
CHOLESTEROL 14MG SODIUM 206MG

EGGPLANT PARMESAN

½ cup dry white wine
1 tablespoon dried basil
1 tablespoon dried oregano
4 (8-ounce) cans no-salt-added tomato sauce
1 (28-ounce) can no-salt-added whole
   tomatoes, undrained and chopped
1 (6-ounce) can tomato paste
2 cloves garlic, minced
2 (1-pound) eggplants, cut crosswise into slices
¼ cup water
3 egg whites, lightly beaten
1¼ cups Italian-seasoned breadcrumbs
¼ cup grated Parmesan cheese
Vegetable cooking spray
3 cups (12 ounces) shredded part-skim
   mozzarella cheese
Fresh oregano sprigs (optional)

Combine first 7 ingredients in a large saucepan; bring to a boil. Reduce heat, and simmer, uncovered, 20 minutes.

Place eggplant in a bowl; add water to cover, and let stand 30 minutes. Drain well; blot dry with paper towels. Combine ¼ cup water and egg whites in a shallow bowl. Combine breadcrumbs and Parmesan cheese; stir well. Dip eggplant in egg white mixture; dredge in breadcrumb mixture.

Place half of eggplant on a baking sheet coated with cooking spray, and broil 5½ inches from heat (with electric oven door partially opened) 5 minutes on each side or until browned. Repeat procedure with remaining eggplant. Set eggplant aside.

Spread half of tomato mixture in a 13- x 9- x 2-inch baking dish coated with cooking spray. Top with half of eggplant and half of mozzarella. Repeat layers. Bake at 350° for 30 minutes or until bubbly. Let stand 5 minutes before serving. Garnish with oregano sprigs, if desired. Yield: 8 servings.

PER SERVING: 298 CALORIES (26% FROM FAT)
FAT 8.5G (SATURATED FAT 5.0G)
PROTEIN 19.2G   CARBOHYDRATE 38.8G
CHOLESTEROL 27MG   SODIUM 818MG

Eggplant Parmesan

SPANAKOPITA QUICHE

Spinach, feta cheese, and phyllo—the key ingredients in the classic Greek dish spanakopita (span-uh-KOH-pih-tuh)—combine with cottage cheese in this unusual quiche. Sprinkle breadcrumbs between the phyllo layers to prevent a soggy crust.

Vegetable cooking spray
1 (10-ounce) package frozen chopped spinach, thawed and drained
1 cup 1% low-fat cottage cheese
½ cup (2 ounces) crumbled feta cheese
⅔ cup nonfat buttermilk
¼ teaspoon pepper
2 eggs
1 egg white
¼ cup chopped green onions
1 tablespoon chopped fresh oregano
1 large clove garlic
6 sheets frozen phyllo pastry, thawed
2 tablespoons fine, dry breadcrumbs, divided
1½ cups (¼-inch-thick) sliced plum tomato

Coat a 9-inch pieplate with cooking spray; set aside. Press spinach between paper towels until barely moist; set aside.

Position knife blade in food processor bowl; add cottage cheese and next 5 ingredients, and process until smooth. Add spinach, green onions, oregano, and garlic; process 45 seconds. Set aside.

Working with 1 phyllo sheet at a time, lightly coat each sheet with cooking spray. Fold phyllo sheet in half crosswise to form a 13- x 8½-inch rectangle, and lightly coat both sides of rectangle with cooking spray. Gently press rectangle into pieplate, allowing ends to extend over edges of pieplate. Repeat procedure with a second sheet of phyllo, placing it across first sheet in a crisscross design; sprinkle 1 tablespoon breadcrumbs over second sheet. Repeat procedure with remaining phyllo and breadcrumbs, continuing in crisscross design, ending with phyllo. Fold in edges of phyllo to fit pieplate and form a rim.

Pour spinach mixture into prepared crust; gently arrange tomato slices over filling. Bake at 350° for 55 minutes or until a knife inserted 1 inch from center comes out clean; let stand 10 minutes. To serve, cut into 6 wedges. Yield: 6 servings.

PER SERVING: 198 CALORIES (27% FROM FAT)
FAT 6.0G (SATURATED FAT 2.5G)
PROTEIN 14.1G   CARBOHYDRATE 22.7G
CHOLESTEROL 85MG   SODIUM 377MG

WEST COAST BREAKFAST BURRITOS

½ cup seeded, chopped tomato
1 tablespoon chopped green onions
1 tablespoon cold water
1 teaspoon chopped jalapeño pepper
2 teaspoons lime juice
⅛ teaspoon dried oregano
Vegetable cooking spray
½ cup frozen egg substitute, thawed
¼ cup diced ripe avocado
¼ cup nonfat sour cream
2 tablespoons canned chopped green chiles, drained
¼ cup (1 ounce) shredded reduced-fat Monterey Jack cheese
2 (10-inch) flour tortillas, heated

Combine first 6 ingredients in a small bowl; set aside.

Coat a small nonstick skillet with cooking spray; place over medium heat until hot. Pour egg substitute into skillet. As mixture begins to cook, gently lift edges of omelet with a spatula, and tilt pan to allow uncooked portion to flow underneath. When set, add avocado, sour cream, chiles, and cheese; stir gently until cheese melts.

Spoon egg substitute mixture evenly down center of each tortilla. Roll up tortillas, folding in sides. Place a tortilla, seam side down, on each of 2 serving plates. Top evenly with tomato mixture. Yield: 2 servings.

PER SERVING: 242 CALORIES (30% FROM FAT)
FAT 8.0G (SATURATED FAT 2.4G)
PROTEIN 15.9G   CARBOHYDRATE 26.1G
CHOLESTEROL 9MG   SODIUM 418MG

Huevos Rancheros

HUEVOS RANCHEROS

1 (14.5-ounce) can no-salt-added whole
   tomatoes, undrained and chopped
1 (15-ounce) can no-salt-added black beans,
   rinsed and drained
1 (4.5-ounce) can chopped green chiles,
   undrained
2 tablespoons chopped fresh cilantro
2 teaspoons chili powder
½ teaspoon ground cumin
¼ teaspoon salt
⅛ teaspoon pepper
2 eggs
2 tablespoons (½ ounce) shredded reduced-fat
   sharp Cheddar cheese
2 tablespoons chopped green onions
Fresh cilantro sprigs (optional)
Fresh jalapeño peppers (optional)

Combine first 8 ingredients in a large nonstick skillet; stir well, and bring to a boil. Cover, reduce heat, and simmer 10 minutes.

Break each egg into a custard cup, and slip eggs from cups into tomato mixture. Cover and simmer 6 minutes or until eggs are done. Remove eggs with a slotted spoon.

Spoon half of tomato mixture onto each of 2 plates, and top with eggs. Sprinkle 1 tablespoon cheese and 1 tablespoon green onions over each serving. Garnish with fresh cilantro sprigs and jalapeño peppers, if desired. Yield: 2 servings.

PER SERVING: 277 CALORIES (23% FROM FAT)
FAT 7.2G (SATURATED FAT 2.5G)
PROTEIN 19.2G   CARBOHYDRATE 35.0G
CHOLESTEROL 226MG   SODIUM 483MG

STACKED RICE AND CHEESE ENCHILADAS

In some areas of New Mexico, enchiladas are served flat instead of rolled around a filling.

1 tablespoon fresh lime juice
8 (¼-inch-thick) slices tomato, halved
1½ teaspoons minced fresh cilantro
1 clove garlic
1 (15-ounce) can no-salt-added black beans, drained
½ cup canned vegetable broth, undiluted
¾ cup cooked long-grain rice (cooked without salt or fat)
¼ cup 1% low-fat cottage cheese
2 tablespoons nonfat sour cream
2 tablespoons finely chopped onion
2 ounces Monterey Jack cheese with peppers, cut into ¼-inch cubes
4 (10-inch) flour tortillas
Vegetable cooking spray

Brush lime juice over tomato slices; sprinkle with cilantro. Cover and chill.

Position knife blade in food processor bowl. Drop garlic through food chute with processor running. Process 3 seconds or until garlic is minced. Add beans and vegetable broth; process until smooth, scraping sides of processor bowl once. Transfer bean mixture to a medium saucepan. Cook, uncovered, over low heat 5 minutes or until slightly thickened, stirring frequently. Set aside; keep warm.

Combine rice, cottage cheese, sour cream, onion, and cubed cheese in a bowl, stirring well. Set rice mixture aside.

Place 2 tortillas on a large baking sheet. Coat tortillas with cooking spray. Broil 3 inches from heat (with electric oven door partially opened) 1 minute or until golden. Remove from oven; set aside, and keep warm. Repeat procedure with remaining tortillas.

Place 1 tortilla, browned side up, on a 12-inch round glass platter; top with about ⅓ cup rice mixture, spreading to edges. Repeat layers twice with 2 tortillas and remaining rice mixture. Top with remaining tortilla. Microwave at HIGH 2 minutes or until cheese melts, rotating platter once.

Remove from microwave, and cut into 4 wedges. Top each wedge with ⅓ cup bean mixture and 4 halved tomato slices. Serve immediately. Yield: 4 servings.

PER SERVING: 315 CALORIES (23% FROM FAT)
FAT 8.1G (SATURATED FAT 3.3G)
PROTEIN 14.0G   CARBOHYDRATE 46.7G
CHOLESTEROL 12MG   SODIUM 437MG

VEGETARIAN PAELLA

Here's a takeoff on the classic Spanish dish with saffron-flavored rice, minus the shellfish, chicken, and sausage. If you want to stick with tradition, include grilled shrimp or fish in the menu.

Vegetable cooking spray
⅔ cup chopped onion
⅔ cup diced sweet red pepper
2 cloves garlic, minced
1 cup frozen artichoke hearts, thawed
1½ cups tightly packed torn fresh spinach
½ cup water
2 (10½-ounce) cans low-salt chicken broth
1¼ cups uncooked jasmine rice
¾ teaspoon salt
½ teaspoon Hungarian sweet paprika
¼ teaspoon threads of saffron
1 cup frozen baby lima beans, thawed
⅓ cup frozen English peas, thawed

Coat a large saucepan with cooking spray, and place over medium-high heat until hot. Add onion, red pepper, and garlic, and sauté 3 minutes. Add artichokes; sauté 2 minutes.

Add spinach, water, and broth to onion mixture; bring to a boil. Stir in rice and next 3 ingredients. Cover, reduce heat, and simmer 15 minutes. Stir in lima beans and peas; cover and cook 10 additional minutes or until liquid is absorbed. Remove from heat; let stand, covered, 5 minutes. Fluff with a fork. Yield: 4 (1¾-cup) servings.

PER SERVING: 348 CALORIES (5% FROM FAT)
FAT 2.1G (SATURATED FAT 0.5G)
PROTEIN 11.9G   CARBOHYDRATE 71.1G
CHOLESTEROL 0MG   SODIUM 607MG

ITALIAN RISOTTO WITH ROASTED RED PEPPERS

Arborio rice is a must for risotto, an Italian dish featuring creamy, broth-cooked rice.

3 large sweet red peppers
2 cups canned vegetable broth, undiluted
2 cups water
1 teaspoon olive oil
1 cup Arborio rice, uncooked
1 (10-ounce) package frozen English peas, thawed
¼ cup freshly grated Parmesan cheese
3 tablespoons chopped fresh basil
3 tablespoons chopped fresh parsley
1 tablespoon lemon juice
⅛ teaspoon freshly ground pepper

Cut peppers in half lengthwise; remove and discard seeds and membranes. Place peppers, skin side up, on a baking sheet, and flatten with palm of hand. Broil 5½ inches from heat (with electric oven door partially opened) 15 to 20 minutes or until charred. Place in ice water until cool; peel and discard skins. Chop and set aside.

Combine broth and water in a saucepan; place over medium heat. Cover and bring to a simmer; reduce heat to low, and keep warm. (Do not boil.)

Heat oil in a medium saucepan over medium-high heat until hot; add rice. Cook, stirring constantly, 2 minutes or until rice is lightly browned. Reduce heat to medium-low.

Add 1 cup of simmering broth mixture to rice, stirring constantly until most of liquid is absorbed. Add remaining broth mixture, ½ cup at a time, cooking and stirring constantly until each ½ cup addition is absorbed (about 30 minutes). (Rice will be tender and will have a creamy consistency.)

Add peas; cook, stirring constantly, until thoroughly heated. Add chopped pepper, cheese, and remaining ingredients; cook, stirring constantly, until thoroughly heated. Yield: 4 (1½-cup) servings.

PER SERVING: 308 CALORIES (11% FROM FAT)
FAT 3.8G (SATURATED FAT 1.0G)
PROTEIN 10.3G   CARBOHYDRATE 56.4G
CHOLESTEROL 4MG   SODIUM 643MG

Roasting Peppers

Place peppers, skin side up, on a baking sheet, and flatten with palm of hand.

Remove roasted peppers from baking sheet; plunge them into ice water until cool.

Peel and discard the blackened skins. The roasted pepper will be soft and slippery.

Vegetable Garden Couscous

VEGETABLE GARDEN COUSCOUS

2 (14½-ounce) cans vegetable broth
4 small round red potatoes, peeled and
    quartered
4 medium carrots, scraped and cut into
    1½-inch pieces
Vegetable cooking spray
1 tablespoon margarine
1 large onion, chopped
2 large cloves garlic, minced
1 teaspoon ground ginger
½ teaspoon ground turmeric
½ teaspoon ground cumin
¼ teaspoon ground cinnamon
3 tablespoons all-purpose flour

1 tablespoon commercial harissa
4 ounces fresh green beans, halved diagonally
1 large sweet red pepper, seeded and cut into
    1-inch pieces
3 tablespoons raisins
2 small zucchini, cut into ½-inch pieces
½ teaspoon salt, divided
¼ teaspoon pepper
¼ cup chopped fresh parsley
¼ cup chopped fresh cilantro
2 tablespoons fresh lemon juice
1 cup couscous, uncooked
2 tablespoons sliced almonds, toasted
Additional harissa (optional)

Combine first 3 ingredients in a large saucepan. Bring to a boil; cover, reduce heat, and simmer 15 minutes or until tender. Remove vegetables with a slotted spoon; keep warm. Reserve 3 cups broth, and set aside.

Coat a large nonstick skillet with cooking spray; add margarine. Place over medium heat until margarine melts. Add onion, and sauté 3 to 5 minutes or until tender. Add garlic; sauté 30 seconds.

Add ginger and next 4 ingredients; stir well. (Mixture will be dry.) Gradually add 1½ cups of reserved broth, stirring constantly. Cook, stirring constantly, 2 minutes or until thickened and bubbly. Stir in 1 tablespoon harissa.

Add beans, sweet red pepper, and raisins. Bring to a boil; cover, reduce heat, and simmer 5 minutes or until beans are tender. Add zucchini and reserved potato and carrot. Cook, covered, 5 minutes or until zucchini is tender. Add ¼ teaspoon salt, pepper, and next 3 ingredients; stir mixture well.

Bring remaining 1½ cups broth and remaining ¼ teaspoon salt to a boil in a medium saucepan; stir in couscous. Remove from heat; cover and let stand 5 minutes. Fluff couscous with a fork. Divide couscous among 4 individual serving plates. Spoon vegetable mixture over couscous; sprinkle evenly with almonds. Serve with additional harissa, if desired. Yield: 4 servings.

PER SERVING: 411 CALORIES (16% FROM FAT)
FAT 7.2G (SATURATED FAT 1.0G)
PROTEIN 11.4G CARBOHYDRATE 81.4G
CHOLESTEROL 0MG SODIUM 837MG

Hot Harissa

Harissa is a hot, red chile paste often served as a condiment with couscous. The heat comes from dried red chiles, which are soaked and ground into paste with a mortar and pestle or in a food processor.

Stir a small amount of harissa into nonfat mayonnaise to serve with fish, or add it to soups, stews, or tomato sauce for extra zip.

FOUR-CHEESE MANICOTTI

12 uncooked manicotti shells
Vegetable cooking spray
½ cup finely chopped onion
3 cloves garlic, minced
1 cup (4 ounces) shredded part-skim
    mozzarella cheese, divided
½ cup freshly grated Parmesan cheese, divided
1 (15-ounce) carton nonfat ricotta cheese
6 ounces garden vegetable-flavored light cream
    cheese, softened
4 ounces block nonfat cream cheese, softened
1 teaspoon dried Italian seasoning
½ teaspoon pepper
½ (10-ounce) package frozen chopped spinach,
    thawed, drained, and squeezed dry
1 (27.5-ounce) jar reduced-fat, reduced-sodium
    tomato-and-herb pasta sauce
Fresh oregano sprigs (optional)

Cook pasta according to package directions, omitting salt and fat; set aside. Coat a small nonstick skillet with cooking spray, and place over medium-high heat until hot. Add onion and garlic; sauté 3 minutes. Remove from heat; set aside.

Combine ½ cup mozzarella, ¼ cup Parmesan, ricotta cheese, and next 4 ingredients in a bowl; beat at medium speed of an electric mixer until smooth. Stir in onion mixture and spinach. Spoon about ⅓ cup cheese mixture into each cooked shell.

Divide 1 cup pasta sauce evenly between 6 individual casserole dishes coated with cooking spray. Arrange 2 stuffed shells in each dish; pour remaining sauce over each. Place dishes on a baking sheet. Cover each dish with foil, and bake at 350° for 25 minutes. Sprinkle with remaining ½ cup mozzarella and ¼ cup Parmesan cheeses; bake, uncovered, 5 minutes. Garnish with oregano sprigs, if desired. Yield: 6 servings.

Note: If you don't have individual casseroles, use a 13- x 9- x 2-inch baking dish to prepare this entrée.

PER SERVING: 386 CALORIES (27% FROM FAT)
FAT 11.7G (SATURATED FAT 6.9G)
PROTEIN 30.0G CARBOHYDRATE 41.5G
CHOLESTEROL 49MG SODIUM 1012MG

Fresh Vegetable Lasagna

FRESH VEGETABLE LASAGNA

2 cups broccoli flowerets
1 cup thinly sliced zucchini
1 cup thinly sliced yellow squash
1 cup thinly sliced carrot
Vegetable cooking spray
1½ cups thinly sliced fresh mushrooms
1 cup chopped onion
3 cups no-salt-added tomato sauce
1 teaspoon garlic powder
1 teaspoon dried Italian seasoning
1 teaspoon dried basil
¾ to 1 teaspoon pepper
½ teaspoon salt
1 (16-ounce) carton 1% low-fat cottage cheese
½ cup frozen egg substitute, thawed
8 cooked lasagna noodles (cooked without salt
    or fat)
1 cup (4 ounces) shredded part-skim
    mozzarella cheese

Arrange first 4 ingredients in a steamer basket over boiling water. Cover and steam 4 to 5 minutes or until vegetables are crisp-tender; drain. Transfer to a bowl; set aside.

Coat a nonstick skillet with cooking spray. Place skillet over medium-high heat until hot. Add mushrooms and onion; sauté until tender. Add to broccoli mixture.

Combine tomato sauce and next 5 ingredients in a small bowl, stirring well. Combine cottage cheese and egg substitute, stirring well.

Spread ½ cup tomato sauce mixture over bottom of a 13- x 9- x 2-inch baking dish coated with cooking spray. Place 4 lasagna noodles over sauce; top evenly with vegetable mixture. Spoon cottage cheese mixture evenly over vegetable mixture. Top with remaining 4 noodles and remaining tomato sauce mixture.

Cover and bake at 350° for 40 minutes. Uncover

and sprinkle with mozzarella cheese. Bake, uncovered, 10 additional minutes or until cheese melts. Let lasagna stand 15 minutes before serving. Yield: 8 servings.

PER SERVING: 234 CALORIES (14% FROM FAT)
FAT 3.6G (SATURATED FAT 1.9G)
PROTEIN 17.7G   CARBOHYDRATE 33.5G
CHOLESTEROL 10MG   SODIUM 500MG

PESTO-STUFFED PASTA SHELLS

(pictured on page 90)

You can purchase pesto sauce instead of making your own. Just be aware that commercial pesto is high in fat.

2 (10-ounce) packages frozen chopped
    spinach, thawed
½ cup Pesto Sauce
2 cups 1% low-fat cottage cheese
3 tablespoons freshly grated Parmesan cheese,
    divided
⅛ teaspoon pepper
⅛ teaspoon freshly grated nutmeg
20 jumbo pasta shells, uncooked
2¼ cups Herbed Tomato Sauce
Vegetable cooking spray
Fresh basil sprigs (optional)

Drain spinach, and press between paper towels to remove excess moisture. Combine spinach, Pesto Sauce, cottage cheese, 2 tablespoons Parmesan cheese, pepper, and nutmeg; stir well.

Cook pasta shells according to package directions, omitting salt and fat; drain. Stuff cheese mixture evenly into cooked shells.

Spoon 1 cup Herbed Tomato Sauce into a 13- x 9- x 2-inch baking dish coated with cooking spray. Place filled shells over sauce. Pour remaining Herbed Tomato Sauce over shells. Cover and bake at 375° for 20 minutes or until hot and bubbly. Remove from oven, and sprinkle with remaining 1 tablespoon Parmesan cheese. Garnish with basil, if desired. Serve immediately. Yield: 5 servings.

PESTO SAUCE

4 cloves garlic
2 tablespoons pine nuts
1½ cups tightly packed fresh basil leaves
½ cup chopped fresh parsley
⅓ cup freshly grated Parmesan cheese
½ cup commercial oil-free Italian dressing

Position knife blade in food processor bowl. Drop garlic and pine nuts through food chute with processor running; process 5 seconds or until garlic is minced. Add basil and parsley; process 10 seconds or until minced. Add cheese; process until blended.

Slowly pour Italian dressing through food chute with processor running, blending until smooth. Yield: 1 cup plus 2 tablespoons.

Note: Remaining Pesto Sauce may be refrigerated for up to 1 week or frozen for longer storage. Spread on chicken or fish before cooking, use as a stuffing for mushroom caps, spread on fresh tomato slices or baguette slices, or serve on hot pasta.

HERBED TOMATO SAUCE

1 teaspoon olive oil
1 cup chopped onion
1 large clove garlic, minced
¼ cup chopped fresh basil
1 tablespoon chopped fresh oregano
½ teaspoon fennel seeds, crushed
1 (14.5-ounce) can no-salt-added whole
    tomatoes, undrained and chopped
½ cup water
1 tablespoon no-salt-added tomato paste
⅛ teaspoon salt
⅛ teaspoon pepper

Heat oil in a medium saucepan over medium-high heat until hot. Add onion and garlic; cook, stirring constantly, 4 minutes or until tender. Add basil, oregano, and fennel seeds; cook, stirring constantly, 1 minute. Add tomatoes and remaining ingredients; bring to a boil. Reduce heat, and simmer, uncovered, 15 minutes. Serve with pasta. Yield: 2¼ cups.

PER SERVING: 365 CALORIES (19% FROM FAT)
FAT 7.6G (SATURATED FAT 2.9G)
PROTEIN 25.3G   CARBOHYDRATE 49.2G
CHOLESTEROL 11MG   SODIUM 800MG

Peasant-Style Green Beans (recipe on page 113)

SALADS & SIDE DISHES

Recipes for regional salads and side dishes are as varied as the people themselves. In China, cooks add soy sauce and ginger to their vegetables, while the French use liberal amounts of garlic and olive oil. A salad in Thailand might contain shallots, cucumber, and rice vinegar, while one in the southwestern United States could feature jicama and corn.

This chapter starts with fruit and vegetable salads (pages 108 through 112) followed by several vegetable side dishes. Be sure to turn to page 116 for the low-fat version of fried green tomatoes, a specialty of the Deep South. And every region has its favorite starchy food. Beginning on page 118, you will find recipes for grits, rice, pasta, and polenta.

Mexican Fruit Salad

MEXICAN FRUIT SALAD

Lime Dressing
1 small head romaine lettuce, shredded
3 large oranges, peeled and sliced crosswise
1 papaya, peeled, seeded, and thinly sliced
2 cups fresh pineapple chunks
1 cup fresh strawberries, hulled
⅓ cup flaked coconut
1 tablespoon pine nuts, toasted

Prepare Lime Dressing.
Place shredded lettuce on a large serving platter. Arrange orange slices, papaya slices, pineapple chunks, and strawberries over lettuce. Sprinkle with coconut and pine nuts. Drizzle Lime Dressing over salad. Serve immediately. Yield: 8 servings.

LIME DRESSING
¾ cup sugar
3 tablespoons water
¾ teaspoon grated lime rind
Juice of 1 large lime

Combine sugar and water in a small saucepan; bring to a boil, stirring constantly until sugar dissolves. Remove from heat; stir in lime rind and juice. Let dressing cool; cover and chill thoroughly. Yield: ¾ cup.

PER SERVING: 175 CALORIES (12% FROM FAT)
FAT 2.3G (SATURATED FAT 1.3G)
PROTEIN 2.0G CARBOHYDRATE 39.0G
CHOLESTEROL 0MG SODIUM 15MG

CREAMY CAESAR SALAD WITH SPICY CROUTONS

1 clove garlic, halved
½ cup nonfat mayonnaise
2 tablespoons red wine vinegar
2 teaspoons Dijon mustard
2 teaspoons white wine Worcestershire sauce
1 teaspoon anchovy paste
¼ teaspoon pepper
2 teaspoons olive oil
¾ teaspoon Cajun seasoning
1 clove garlic, minced
2 cups (¾-inch) sourdough bread cubes
18 cups torn romaine lettuce
⅓ cup freshly grated Parmesan cheese

Drop 1 clove garlic through food chute of a food processor with processor running; process until garlic is minced. Add mayonnaise and next 5 ingredients; process until blended. Cover and chill 1 hour.
Combine oil, Cajun seasoning, and minced garlic in a medium microwave-safe bowl. Microwave at HIGH 20 seconds. Add bread cubes; toss gently to coat. Spread bread cubes in a single layer on a baking sheet; bake at 400° for 15 minutes or until golden brown.
Place lettuce in a large bowl. Add dressing; toss gently to coat. Sprinkle with cheese, and top with croutons. Yield: 6 servings.

PER SERVING: 137 CALORIES (27% FROM FAT)
FAT 4.1G (SATURATED FAT 1.3G)
PROTEIN 7.7G CARBOHYDRATE 18.2G
CHOLESTEROL 4MG SODIUM 836MG

Fat Alert

Ordering a Caesar salad in a restaurant can be as entertaining as it is delicious. The waiter dramatically prepares the salad at your table, starting with romaine and a gracious amount of olive oil. He cracks a raw egg into the greens, adds anchovies and Parmesan, and tosses it all together.

Obviously this classic salad can be high in fat. But in the above recipe, the fat is reduced by decreasing the oil and adding nonfat mayonnaise and vinegar. A small amount of anchovy paste replaces whole anchovies. To prevent a potential risk of food poisoning, the raw egg is omitted.

Spinach-Garbanzo Salad with Guacamole Dressing

SPINACH-GARBANZO SALAD WITH GUACAMOLE DRESSING

The fat in this Mexican-style guacamole is reduced by stretching the high-fat avocado with evaporated skimmed milk and nonfat sour cream.

Guacamole Dressing
5½ cups shredded iceberg lettuce
3 cups tightly packed shredded fresh spinach
1 (15-ounce) can garbanzo beans, drained
1 (14.4-ounce) can hearts of palm, drained and cut into ¾-inch slices
¾ cup chopped sweet red pepper
2 ounces small fresh spinach leaves

Prepare Guacamole Dressing.

Combine lettuce and next 4 ingredients in a large bowl; toss well.

Arrange spinach leaves evenly on 8 individual salad plates. Spoon lettuce mixture evenly over spinach leaves. Spoon Guacamole Dressing evenly over salads. Serve immediately. Yield: 8 (1½-cup) servings.

GUACAMOLE DRESSING

¾ cup peeled, chopped avocado
¼ cup evaporated skimmed milk
1½ tablespoons lemon juice
1 tablespoon nonfat sour cream
½ teaspoon chili powder
¼ teaspoon Worcestershire sauce
⅛ teaspoon ground cumin
1 large clove garlic, crushed

Combine all ingredients in container of an electric blender; cover and process until smooth, stopping once to scrape down sides. Cover and chill thoroughly. Yield: 1 cup.

PER SERVING: 143 CALORIES (26% FROM FAT)
FAT 4.1G (SATURATED FAT 0.6G)
PROTEIN 6.7G   CARBOHYDRATE 23.0G
CHOLESTEROL 0MG   SODIUM 190MG

STEAMED ANTIPASTO

Literally meaning "before the pasta," antipasto can be served as an appetizer or as a salad with an Italian dinner.

3 medium-size fresh beets (about 1 pound)
2 cups (2-inch) julienne-sliced carrot
2 cups cauliflower flowerets
¾ cup commercial oil-free Italian dressing, divided
2 ounces reduced-fat Monterey Jack cheese, cut into ½-inch cubes
5 fresh spinach leaves
10 cherry tomatoes, halved
10 pickled banana peppers

Leave root and 1 inch of stem on beets; scrub with a brush. Arrange in a steamer basket over boiling water in a Dutch oven. Cover and steam 30 minutes. (Add boiling water to pan, if needed.) Trim off stems and roots; rub off skins. Cut beets into ½-inch cubes; set aside.

Arrange carrot and cauliflower in steamer basket over boiling water. Cover and steam 5 minutes. Rinse under cold, running water. Set aside.

Combine beets and ¼ cup dressing in a large heavy-duty, zip-top plastic bag. Seal bag, and marinate in refrigerator 8 hours.

Combine remaining ½ cup dressing, carrot, cauliflower, and cheese in a large heavy-duty, zip-top plastic bag. Seal bag, and marinate in refrigerator 8 hours.

Drain vegetable mixtures, discarding marinade. Combine beets and carrot mixture; toss gently. Divide evenly among 5 spinach-lined salad plates. Arrange tomato halves and banana peppers on each salad. Yield: 5 servings.

PER SERVING: 115 CALORIES (23% FROM FAT)
FAT 2.9G (SATURATED FAT 1.3G)
PROTEIN 6.4G   CARBOHYDRATE 18.2G
CHOLESTEROL 7MG   SODIUM 396MG

SOUTHWESTERN CORN AND PEPPER SALAD

1¾ cups fresh corn cut from cob
1½ cups water
¾ cup diced green pepper
¾ cup diced sweet red pepper
¾ cup peeled, diced jicama
¼ cup diced purple onion
3 tablespoons sliced ripe olives
2 tablespoons minced fresh cilantro
2½ tablespoons balsamic vinegar
1 teaspoon sugar
1 teaspoon olive oil
½ teaspoon ground coriander
½ teaspoon ground cumin
¼ teaspoon salt
⅛ teaspoon pepper

Combine corn and water in a saucepan. Bring to a boil; cover, reduce heat, and simmer 20 minutes or until tender. Drain and let cool.

Combine corn, green pepper, and remaining ingredients in a large bowl, tossing well. Cover and chill at least 2 hours. Yield: 4 (1-cup) servings.

PER SERVING: 104 CALORIES (27% FROM FAT)
FAT 3.1G (SATURATED FAT 0.5G)
PROTEIN 2.9G CARBOHYDRATE 19.3G
CHOLESTEROL 0MG SODIUM 238MG

THAI CUCUMBER SALAD

⅓ cup minced shallots
⅓ cup sliced green onions
4 medium cucumbers (about 2½ pounds),
    peeled, halved lengthwise, seeded, and
    thinly sliced
2 to 4 small hot red chiles, halved lengthwise,
    seeded, and thinly sliced (about 1 to 2
    tablespoons)
½ cup rice vinegar
2 tablespoons sugar
½ teaspoon salt
¼ cup chopped fresh cilantro

Combine first 4 ingredients in a large bowl. Combine vinegar, sugar, and salt, and stir well. Add to cucumber mixture, tossing to coat. Stir in fresh cilantro. Yield: 10 (½-cup) servings.

PER SERVING: 30 CALORIES (3% FROM FAT)
FAT 0.1G (SATURATED FAT 0.0G)
PROTEIN 0.8G CARBOHYDRATE 6.8G
CHOLESTEROL 0MG SODIUM 126MG

MED-RIM TABBOULEH

Tabbouleh is the signature cracked-wheat salad of many Arabic countries. Here it's highlighted with almonds and calls for pomegranate molasses, which adds an interesting taste to the dish.

1½ cups uncooked bulgur (cracked wheat)
1½ cups boiling water
1 teaspoon olive oil
1½ cups diced onion
¾ cup finely chopped fresh parsley
⅓ cup finely chopped fresh cilantro
¼ cup slivered almonds, toasted
1 tablespoon ground cumin
3 tablespoons fresh lemon juice
2 teaspoons olive oil
1 tablespoon pomegranate molasses
1½ teaspoons dried oregano
½ teaspoon salt
⅛ teaspoon ground allspice

Combine bulgur and boiling water in a large bowl; stir well. Cover and let stand 30 minutes or until water is absorbed.

Heat 1 teaspoon oil in a small skillet over medium heat. Add onion; sauté 5 minutes or until tender. Add cooked onion to bulgur; stir in parsley and remaining ingredients. Cover and chill. Yield: 4 (1-cup) servings.

PER SERVING: 285 CALORIES (25% FROM FAT)
FAT 7.8G (SATURATED FAT 1.0G)
PROTEIN 9.2G CARBOHYDRATE 49.6G
CHOLESTEROL 0MG SODIUM 316MG

PEASANT-STYLE GREEN BEANS

(pictured on page 106)

Two flavors of southern French cooking—olive oil and garlic—give this simple summer vegetable a foreign accent.

1 pound fresh green beans
2 teaspoons olive oil
1 cup chopped onion
2 cloves garlic, crushed
1 (14½-ounce) can no-salt-added whole tomatoes, drained and chopped
⅓ cup dry red wine
½ teaspoon dried oregano
½ teaspoon pepper

Wash beans; trim ends, and remove strings. Arrange beans in a steamer basket over boiling water. Cover and steam 5 minutes or until crisp-tender. Set aside, and keep warm.

Heat oil in a large nonstick skillet over medium-high heat until hot. Add onion and garlic; sauté until tender. Add tomatoes and remaining 3 ingredients. Cook over low heat 15 minutes, stirring occasionally. Remove from heat; add beans, tossing well to combine. Yield: 7 (½-cup) servings.

PER SERVING: 50 CALORIES (25% FROM FAT)
FAT 1.4G (SATURATED FAT 0.2G)
PROTEIN 1.9G CARBOHYDRATE 9.0G
CHOLESTEROL 0MG SODIUM 10MG

BOSTON BAKED BEANS

1 pound dried Great Northern beans
5 cups water
2 cups chopped onion
1¼ cups (6 ounces) finely cubed, cooked lean ham
½ cup dark molasses
1 tablespoon plus 2 teaspoons dry mustard
½ teaspoon salt
½ teaspoon pepper

Sort and wash beans; place in a large Dutch oven. Cover with water 2 inches above beans, and bring to a boil; cook 2 minutes. Remove from heat; cover and let stand 1 hour.

Drain beans. Combine beans, 5 cups water, and remaining ingredients in a 3-quart casserole. Cover and bake at 350° for 3 hours, stirring occasionally. Uncover and bake 1½ additional hours or until beans are tender, stirring occasionally. Yield: 16 (½-cup) servings.

Note: Freeze extra servings in an airtight container up to 3 months. Thaw overnight in refrigerator. To serve, place beans in a saucepan, and cook over medium heat until thoroughly heated, stirring beans occasionally.

PER SERVING: 148 CALORIES (7% FROM FAT)
FAT 1.2G (SATURATED FAT 0.3G)
PROTEIN 8.6G CARBOHYDRATE 26.7G
CHOLESTEROL 6MG SODIUM 209MG

Boston Baked Beans

ORIENTAL BROCCOLI

1½ pounds fresh broccoli
3 tablespoons low-sodium soy sauce
2 teaspoons dark sesame oil
1 teaspoon honey
½ teaspoon peeled, grated gingerroot
    or ¼ teaspoon ground ginger
¼ teaspoon dry mustard
8 small cherry tomatoes, halved
½ cup sliced water chestnuts
2 green onions, diagonally sliced

Trim off large leaves of broccoli, and remove tough ends of lower stalks. Wash broccoli thoroughly, and coarsely chop. Arrange in a vegetable steamer over boiling water. Cover and steam 5 to 8 minutes or until crisp-tender. Drain; transfer to a serving bowl, and keep warm.

Combine soy sauce and next 4 ingredients in a small saucepan; stir well. Bring to a boil over medium heat. Pour over broccoli. Add tomatoes, water chestnuts, and green onions; toss gently. Serve immediately. Yield: 6 (1-cup) servings.

PER SERVING: 56 CALORIES (31% FROM FAT)
FAT 1.9G (SATURATED FAT 0.3G)
PROTEIN 3.1G CARBOHYDRATE 8.2G
CHOLESTEROL 0MG SODIUM 223MG

CARROT AND ONION AGRODOLCE

Agrodolce is Italian for "sour-sweet." Italians cook many vegetables this way, serving them as a side dish.

1 tablespoon olive oil
2 cups trimmed, scraped baby carrots
2 peeled medium onions, each cut into 8 wedges
⅓ cup unsweetened apple juice
2 tablespoons raisins
1 tablespoon brown sugar
2 tablespoons fresh lemon juice
½ teaspoon salt
¼ teaspoon rubbed sage
1 lemon, thinly sliced

Heat oil in a large nonstick skillet over medium-high heat. Add carrots and onion; reduce heat to medium, and cook 25 minutes or until onion is golden, stirring frequently. Stir in apple juice and remaining ingredients; cover, reduce heat, and simmer 15 minutes or until carrots are tender, stirring occasionally. Yield: 4 (¾-cup) servings.

Note: True baby carrots are usually sold in a bundle with their green tops intact. They are sweeter than the smaller carrots sold in a bag.

PER SERVING: 124 CALORIES (27% FROM FAT)
FAT 3.7G (SATURATED FAT 0.5G)
PROTEIN 1.9G CARBOHYDRATE 24.6G
CHOLESTEROL 0MG SODIUM 318MG

CARIBBEAN CORN

Vegetable cooking spray
3 cups fresh corn cut from cob (about 6 ears)
1 clove garlic, minced
3 tablespoons unsweetened pineapple juice
3 tablespoons skim milk
½ teaspoon sugar
½ teaspoon ground cumin
¼ teaspoon ground ginger
1½ teaspoons low-sodium soy sauce
¼ cup sliced green onions

Coat a large skillet with cooking spray; place over medium heat until hot. Add corn and garlic; sauté 5 minutes. Combine pineapple juice and next 5 ingredients; add to corn. Cover, reduce heat, and simmer 15 minutes, stirring occasionally. Add green onions; cover and cook 5 additional minutes. Yield: 5 (½-cup) servings.

PER SERVING: 122 CALORIES (10% FROM FAT)
FAT 1.4G (SATURATED FAT 0.2G)
PROTEIN 3.8G CARBOHYDRATE 27.7G
CHOLESTEROL 0MG SODIUM 83MG

Roasted Ratatouille

ROASTED RATATOUILLE

1 (1-pound) unpeeled eggplant, cut crosswise
   into ¾-inch slices
2 teaspoons olive oil, divided
Vegetable cooking spray
3 medium zucchini (about 1 pound), cut
   crosswise into ¾-inch slices
1½ cups vertically sliced onion
2 cloves garlic, crushed
1½ cups (1-inch-square) cut sweet red pepper
1½ cups (1-inch-square) cut green pepper
2 cups seeded, chopped unpeeled tomato
2 tablespoons chopped fresh parsley
½ teaspoon dried thyme
¼ teaspoon salt
⅛ teaspoon pepper

Cut each eggplant slice into 4 wedges; place in a bowl. Drizzle with 1 teaspoon oil, and toss. Arrange eggplant in a single layer on a baking sheet coated with cooking spray. Broil 5½ inches from heat (with electric oven door partially opened) 14 minutes or until browned, turning after 7 minutes; place eggplant in bowl, and set aside.

Place zucchini in a bowl; drizzle with remaining 1 teaspoon oil, and toss well. Arrange zucchini in a single layer on a baking sheet coated with cooking spray. Broil 5½ inches from heat (with electric oven door partially opened) 7 minutes or until browned; add to eggplant, and set aside.

Coat a large nonstick skillet with cooking spray; place over medium heat until hot. Add onion, garlic, and red and green peppers; sauté 10 minutes or until tender. Add tomato; sauté 5 minutes.

Stir in eggplant mixture, parsley, and remaining ingredients. Cover, reduce heat, and simmer 15 minutes. Yield: 6 (1-cup) servings.

PER SERVING: 80 CALORIES (26% FROM FAT)
FAT 2.3G (SATURATED FAT 0.3G)
PROTEIN 2.8G   CARBOHYDRATE 14.7G
CHOLESTEROL 0MG   SODIUM 111MG

Fried Green Tomatoes with Lima-Corn Relish

FRIED GREEN TOMATOES WITH LIMA-CORN RELISH

1 cup frozen baby lima beans, cooked
1 cup frozen whole kernel corn, thawed
½ cup diced sweet red pepper
3 tablespoons thinly sliced fresh basil
2 tablespoons hot pepper sauce
1 tablespoon white wine vinegar
1 teaspoon olive oil
2 cloves garlic, crushed
3 tablespoons yellow cornmeal
2 tablespoons grated Parmesan cheese
⅛ teaspoon salt
⅛ teaspoon pepper
8 (¼-inch-thick) slices green tomato
2 teaspoons olive oil
12 (¼-inch-thick) slices red tomato
Fresh basil sprigs (optional)

Combine first 8 ingredients in a bowl; stir well. Cover and chill 1 hour.

Combine cornmeal and cheese in a small heavy-duty, zip-top plastic bag. Sprinkle salt and pepper over green tomato slices, and place slices, 1 at a time, in cornmeal mixture; seal bag, and shake to coat well.

Heat 2 teaspoons oil in a large nonstick skillet over medium-high heat. Add green tomato slices, and cook 3 minutes on each side or until browned.

Arrange lima bean mixture, fried green tomato slices, and red tomato slices on a serving platter. Garnish with basil sprigs, if desired. Serve immediately. Yield: 4 servings.

PER SERVING: 180 CALORIES (25% FROM FAT)
FAT 5.0G (SATURATED FAT 1.0G)
PROTEIN 7.2G CARBOHYDRATE 29.0G
CHOLESTEROL 2MG SODIUM 253MG

CHAMP

Although the traditional Irish dish calls for butter, low-fat milk does the trick in this version.

2½ cups peeled, cubed Yukon gold or baking
    potato (about 1 pound)
½ cup 1% low-fat milk
¼ cup finely chopped green onions
¼ teaspoon salt
⅛ teaspoon pepper
Vegetable cooking spray

Place potato in a medium saucepan; add water to cover. Bring to a boil, and cook 15 minutes or until very tender; drain in a colander, and set aside.

Combine milk and green onions in pan, and cook over medium heat until thoroughly heated (do not boil). Add potato, salt, and pepper to milk mixture; beat at medium speed of an electric mixer until smooth.

Divide mixture evenly between 2 (8-ounce) ramekins coated with cooking spray; broil 5½ inches from heat (with electric oven door partially opened) 5 minutes or until lightly browned. Yield: 2 servings.

PER SERVING: 180 CALORIES (6% FROM FAT)
FAT 1.2G (SATURATED FAT 0.5G)
PROTEIN 6.6G CARBOHYDRATE 36.9G
CHOLESTEROL 2MG SODIUM 340MG

Soufflé Success

The lightest soufflés start with stiffly beaten egg whites. Separate the eggs while cold, but let them stand at room temperature for 20 minutes before beating the whites. Use only copper, metal, or glass bowls (never plastic), and make sure the bowls and beaters are grease-free.

For stiff peaks, the egg whites will be moist and glossy, and sharp peaks will form when the beaters are removed.

SOUFFLÉ AUX ÉPINARDS

This French dish translates to spinach soufflé in English.

1 (10-ounce) package frozen chopped spinach,
    thawed and drained
Vegetable cooking spray
1 tablespoon minced shallots
1 cup skim milk
1 tablespoon cornstarch
2 eggs, separated
¼ cup (1 ounce) shredded reduced-fat Swiss
    cheese
¼ teaspoon salt
⅛ teaspoon pepper
Dash of ground nutmeg
Dash of ground red pepper
3 egg whites

Press thawed spinach between paper towels until barely moist; set aside. Coat a nonstick skillet with cooking spray; place over medium heat until hot. Add minced shallots, and sauté 1 minute. Add spinach, and sauté 1 minute. Set aside.

Combine milk and cornstarch in a saucepan; stir well. Bring to a boil over low heat, and cook, stirring constantly, 2 minutes. Beat 2 egg yolks until thick and pale. Gradually stir one-fourth of hot mixture into yolks; add to remaining hot mixture, stirring constantly. Cook 1 minute. Add cheese and next 4 ingredients, stirring until cheese melts. Pour mixture into a bowl. Add spinach mixture; stir well.

Beat 5 egg whites at high speed of an electric mixer until stiff peaks form. Stir one-fourth of egg whites into spinach mixture; fold remaining egg whites into spinach mixture.

Spoon mixture into a 6-cup soufflé dish coated with cooking spray. Place on middle rack of a 400° oven; immediately reduce temperature to 375°, and bake 25 minutes. Serve soufflé immediately. Yield: 6 (1-cup) servings.

PER SERVING: 81 CALORIES (32% FROM FAT)
FAT 2.9G (SATURATED FAT 1.1G)
PROTEIN 8.3G CARBOHYDRATE 5.9G
CHOLESTEROL 77MG SODIUM 210MG

SNOW PEA AND CHINESE MUSHROOM STIR-FRY

1 cup boiling water
1 (.75-ounce) package dried black mushrooms
Vegetable cooking spray
2 teaspoons dark sesame oil
1 (8-ounce) can sliced bamboo shoots, drained
5 cups fresh snow pea pods (about 1 pound), trimmed
¼ teaspoon salt
¼ teaspoon sugar

Combine boiling water and mushrooms in a bowl; cover and let stand 15 minutes. Drain mushrooms, reserving 2 tablespoons liquid. Discard mushroom stems; thinly slice mushroom caps, and set aside.

Coat a wok or a large nonstick skillet with cooking spray. Add oil; heat at medium-high (375°) until hot. Add mushrooms and bamboo shoots; stir-fry 2 minutes. Add 2 tablespoons reserved liquid, snow peas, salt, and sugar; stir-fry 2 minutes. Yield: 6 (1-cup) servings.

PER SERVING: 82 CALORIES (20% FROM FAT)
FAT 1.8G (SATURATED FAT 0.3G)
PROTEIN 4.0G CARBOHYDRATE 12.4G
CHOLESTEROL 0MG SODIUM 104MG

Stir-Frying Basics

• Chop, slice, and measure all ingredients before starting. Line up everything you'll need near the cooking surface.

• Make sure vegetables are as dry as possible to keep hot oil from spattering as you add them to the wok.

• Cook in small batches to avoid overcrowding the wok; overcooking means soggy food.

• Always keep food in motion; stir with a wok utensil or wooden spoon as if you were tossing a salad.

CHEESE GRITS WITH GARLIC

Grits, small flakes of dried corn, can be found on breakfast menus across the South.

Vegetable cooking spray
1½ tablespoons chopped onion
1 clove garlic, minced
1¾ cups skim milk
1½ cups water
¾ cup quick-cooking grits, uncooked
1 egg, lightly beaten
1 egg white, lightly beaten
1 cup (4 ounces) shredded reduced-fat sharp Cheddar cheese
¼ teaspoon salt
2¼ teaspoons low-sodium Worcestershire sauce
⅛ teaspoon hot sauce

Coat a large saucepan with cooking spray; place over medium-high heat until hot. Add onion and garlic; sauté until tender. Stir in milk and water; bring to a boil. Stir in grits. Cover, reduce heat, and simmer 5 minutes or until thickened, stirring occasionally. Remove from heat.

Combine egg and remaining 5 ingredients, stirring well. Stir about one-fourth of grits mixture into egg mixture; add to remaining grits mixture, stirring until cheese melts.

Pour grits mixture into a 1½-quart casserole coated with cooking spray. Bake at 350° for 30 to 35 minutes or until set. Yield: 6 servings.

PER SERVING: 168 CALORIES (26% FROM FAT)
FAT 4.8G (SATURATED FAT 2.5G)
PROTEIN 11.4G CARBOHYDRATE 19.7G
CHOLESTEROL 50MG SODIUM 303MG

Easy Spanish Rice

EASY SPANISH RICE

Vegetable cooking spray
½ cup chopped green pepper
½ cup chopped onion
2 (8-ounce) cans no-salt-added tomato sauce
1 (14½-ounce) can no-salt-added stewed
  tomatoes, undrained and chopped
1 cup long-grain rice, uncooked
¼ cup water
1 teaspoon chili powder
½ teaspoon dried oregano
¼ teaspoon salt
¼ teaspoon ground red pepper
¼ teaspoon ground cumin

Coat a large nonstick skillet with cooking spray, and place over medium-high heat until hot. Add green pepper and onion; sauté 5 minutes or until vegetables are tender.

Add tomato sauce and remaining ingredients to vegetables in skillet. Bring mixture to a boil; cover, reduce heat, and simmer 25 to 30 minutes or until rice is tender and liquid is absorbed. Spoon into a serving bowl. Yield: 8 (½-cup) servings.

PER SERVING: 125 CALORIES (2% FROM FAT)
FAT 0.3G (SATURATED FAT 0.1G)
PROTEIN 3.0G CARBOHYDRATE 27.7G
CHOLESTEROL 0MG SODIUM 99MG

POLENTA WITH MUSHROOM-TOMATO SAUCE

You could also serve this Italian dish as a light entrée.

1 cup coarse yellow cornmeal
1 cup cold water
2 cups canned vegetable broth, undiluted
¾ cup frozen whole kernel corn
½ cup freshly grated Parmesan cheese, divided
¼ teaspoon salt
Olive oil-flavored vegetable cooking spray
1 teaspoon olive oil
1 large onion, chopped
1 large clove garlic, minced
⅛ teaspoon dried crushed red pepper
½ pound fresh mushrooms, sliced
⅓ cup dry white wine
1 (14.5-ounce) can no-salt-added whole tomatoes, undrained and chopped
2 tablespoons chopped fresh parsley
1 tablespoon chopped fresh basil
1 tablespoon chopped fresh oregano
¼ teaspoon salt
⅛ teaspoon pepper

Combine cornmeal and water in a small bowl, and set aside.

Pour vegetable broth into a medium saucepan, and bring to a boil over high heat. Add cornmeal mixture in a slow, steady stream, stirring constantly. Stir in corn. Reduce heat to medium; cook, stirring constantly, 20 minutes or until mixture pulls away from sides of pan. Add ¼ cup cheese and ¼ teaspoon salt, stirring until cheese melts. Spoon into an 8-inch round cakepan coated with cooking spray. Set polenta aside; let cool completely.

Coat a large nonstick skillet with cooking spray; add oil. Place over medium-high heat until hot. Add onion; sauté until tender. Add garlic and crushed red pepper; cook 1 minute. Add mushrooms; sauté until tender. Add wine and tomatoes; cook over medium-high heat, stirring constantly, until most of liquid evaporates. Add parsley and remaining 4 ingredients. Set aside; keep warm.

Turn polenta out onto a cutting board; cut into 6 wedges. Place polenta on a baking sheet coated with cooking spray. Coat polenta lightly with cooking spray. Broil 5½ inches from heat (with electric oven door partially opened) 6 minutes or until crusty and golden. Place a polenta wedge on each individual serving plate. Top wedges evenly with mushroom mixture and remaining ¼ cup cheese. Serve warm. Yield: 6 servings.

PER SERVING: 253 CALORIES (23% FROM FAT)
FAT 6.4G (SATURATED FAT 3.0G)
PROTEIN 11.1G   CARBOHYDRATE 37.1G
CHOLESTEROL 11MG   SODIUM 475MG

PASTA WITH GREMOLATA

Gremolata, a combination of parsley, lemon, and garlic, adds a sprightly taste to meats and side dishes.

½ cup packed fresh parsley, finely chopped
½ teaspoon grated lemon rind
2 large cloves garlic, minced
1 tablespoon extra-virgin olive oil, divided
1 (14½-ounce) can plum tomatoes, undrained and chopped
1 tablespoon chopped fresh basil
3 cups cooked penne (short tubular pasta), cooked without salt or fat
Fresh parsley sprigs (optional)

Combine chopped parsley, lemon rind, and garlic; set aside.

Heat 1½ teaspoons oil in a medium skillet over medium heat. Add tomatoes; bring to a boil, and cook 10 minutes. Stir in basil.

Combine pasta and remaining 1½ teaspoons oil in a bowl; toss. Add parsley mixture and tomatoes, tossing gently. Serve warm. Garnish with parsley sprigs, if desired. Yield: 4 (¾-cup) servings.

PER SERVING: 198 CALORIES (20% FROM FAT)
FAT 4.5G (SATURATED FAT 0.6G)
PROTEIN 6.0G   CARBOHYDRATE 34.3G
CHOLESTEROL 0MG   SODIUM 15MG

Pasta with Gremolata

Flan (recipe on page 139)

CLASSIC DESSERTS

*G*o globetrotting through the world's cuisines, and you'll find an incredible variety of flavors and ingredients. Yet people of all regions have one thing in common when it comes to food—a universal sweet tooth. It seems everyone can find a reason to prepare and serve dessert. A Mexican mother might prepare Flan (page 139) for Cinco de Mayo while a Lebanese family enjoys baklava (page 127) on a special holiday. And for almost any occasion, a Southerner will prepare Mississippi Mud Cake (page 124).

Here's a collection of some of our favorite desserts. Cakes start on page 124, followed by cookies and frozen desserts. You'll also find pies, pastries, crêpes, and as a finale, the New Orleans favorite, Bread Pudding with Whiskey Sauce.

MISSISSIPPI MUD CAKE

⅓ cup margarine, softened
1 cup sugar
3 eggs
1 cup all-purpose flour
⅓ cup unsweetened cocoa
½ teaspoon baking powder
¼ teaspoon salt
½ cup chopped pecans
1 teaspoon vanilla extract
Vegetable cooking spray
Chocolate Glaze
3¼ cups miniature marshmallows

Cream margarine, and gradually add sugar, beating at medium speed of an electric mixer until well blended. Add eggs, 1 at a time, beating well after each addition.

Combine flour, cocoa, baking powder, and salt; stir well. Add to margarine mixture, beating at low speed until blended. Stir in pecans and vanilla. Pour batter into a 13- x 9- x 2-inch baking dish coated with cooking spray. Bake at 325° for 16 minutes or just until set. (Do not bake until wooden pick tests clean, or cake will be overbaked). While cake bakes, prepare Chocolate Glaze; set aside.

Remove cake from oven; top with marshmallows. Bake 2 minutes or until marshmallows are soft. Remove from oven; drizzle with Chocolate Glaze, and let cool. Yield: 16 servings.

CHOCOLATE GLAZE
2 cups sifted powdered sugar
¼ cup plus 2 tablespoons unsweetened cocoa
¼ cup skim milk
2 tablespoons margarine
1 teaspoon vanilla extract

Combine sugar and cocoa in a medium bowl; stir. Combine milk and margarine in a 1-cup glass measure. Microwave at HIGH 1 minute. Add milk mixture and vanilla to sugar mixture; beat at low speed of an electric mixer until blended. Yield: 1 cup.

PER SERVING: 271 CALORIES (16% FROM FAT)
FAT 9.4G (SATURATED FAT 1.9G)
PROTEIN 3.8G   CARBOHYDRATE 44.0G
CHOLESTEROL 42MG   SODIUM 118MG

ITALIAN CREAM CAKE

The name is deceiving—this recipe is a favorite in the southern United States, not Italy.

Cream Cheese Icing
Vegetable cooking spray
2 cups sugar
½ cup light butter
2 large egg yolks
2 cups all-purpose flour
1 teaspoon baking soda
1 cup low-fat buttermilk
½ cup chopped pecans
1 teaspoon butter flavoring
1 teaspoon coconut extract
1 teaspoon vanilla extract
6 large egg whites
Lemon rind strips (optional)

Prepare Cream Cheese Icing; cover and chill.

Coat bottoms of 3 (9-inch) round cakepans with cooking spray (do not coat sides of pans); line bottoms of pans with wax paper. Coat wax paper with cooking spray, and dust with flour; set aside.

Combine sugar and butter in a large bowl; beat at medium speed of an electric mixer until well blended. Add egg yolks, 1 at a time, beating well after each addition. Combine 2 cups flour and baking soda; stir well. Add flour mixture to butter mixture alternately with buttermilk, beginning and ending with flour mixture. Stir in pecans and next 3 ingredients.

Beat egg whites at high speed of an electric mixer until stiff peaks form (do not overbeat). Fold egg whites into batter; pour batter into prepared pans. Bake at 350° for 23 minutes. Let cool in pans 5 minutes on wire racks. Loosen cake layers from sides of pans, using a narrow metal spatula, and turn out onto wire racks. Peel off wax paper; let cool completely.

Place 1 cake layer on a plate, and spread with ⅔ cup Cream Cheese Icing; top with another cake layer. Repeat with ⅔ cup icing and remaining layer, ending with cake layer. Spread remaining icing over sides and top of cake. Garnish with lemon rind strips, if desired. Yield: 20 servings.

Italian Cream Cake

CREAM CHEESE ICING

1 tablespoon light butter, chilled
1 (8-ounce) package Neufchâtel cheese, chilled
1 teaspoon vanilla extract
1 (1-pound) package powdered sugar, sifted

Beat butter and cheese at high speed of an electric mixer until fluffy; add vanilla. Gradually add sugar, and beat at low speed just until blended (do not overbeat or icing will become runny). Cover; chill. Yield: 2⅔ cups.

PER SERVING: 300 CALORIES (24% FROM FAT)
FAT 8.0G (SATURATED FAT 3.9G)
PROTEIN 4.5G   CARBOHYDRATE 53.8G
CHOLESTEROL 39MG   SODIUM 166MG

Icing Tips

Follow these tips for making the icing for Italian Cream Cake:
• Chill a glass or metal mixing bowl.
• Use chilled butter and cream cheese straight from the refrigerator.
• Mix the icing only until the sugar is incorporated. Excessive beating "warms up" the cream cheese, making it too soft.
• If it's an exceptionally hot, humid day, set the bowl of icing into a larger bowl of ice water while you frost the cake.

Peach Melba Trifle

1 (5.1-ounce) package vanilla instant pudding
  mix
2 cups skim milk
½ cup light process cream cheese, softened
1 (8-ounce) carton raspberry low-fat yogurt
1 (10½-ounce) loaf commercial angel food
  cake
3 cups sliced fresh peaches
2 cups fresh raspberries
Raspberry Sauce

Combine pudding mix and milk; beat at low
speed of an electric mixer until smooth. Set aside.

Beat cream cheese at medium speed until creamy.
Add yogurt, beating just until blended. Stir in pudding mixture. Cover; chill at least 30 minutes.

Cut cake into 1-inch cubes. Arrange 2 cups cake
cubes in a 3-quart trifle bowl. Spread 1⅓ cups pudding mixture over cake cubes. Arrange 1 cup
peaches over pudding mixture; top with ⅔ cup
raspberries. Repeat layers twice with remaining
cake, pudding mixture, peaches, and raspberries.
Cover and chill at least 3 hours. Serve with
Raspberry Sauce. Yield: 12 servings.

Raspberry Sauce

3 cups fresh raspberries
2 tablespoons Chambord or other raspberry-
  flavored liqueur
1 tablespoon sugar
2 teaspoons cornstarch

Combine raspberries and liqueur in container of
an electric blender; cover and process until smooth.
Place raspberry mixture in a wire-mesh strainer
over a bowl; press with back of spoon against sides
of strainer to squeeze out juice. Discard pulp and
seeds remaining in strainer.

Combine raspberry puree, sugar, and cornstarch
in a saucepan, stirring well. Cook over medium
heat, stirring constantly, until thickened. Remove
from heat; cool completely. Yield: 1½ cups.

PER SERVING: 217 CALORIES (10% FROM FAT)
FAT 2.3G (SATURATED FAT 1.2G)
PROTEIN 5.3G   CARBOHYDRATE 45.6G
CHOLESTEROL 7MG   SODIUM 205MG

Cappuccino Biscotti

*This crunchy Italian cookie is great for dunking
into coffee.*

2 cups all-purpose flour
½ teaspoon baking powder
½ teaspoon baking soda
½ teaspoon salt
½ teaspoon ground cinnamon
1 cup sugar
⅓ cup chopped walnuts
¼ cup unsweetened cocoa
2 teaspoons instant coffee granules
2 teaspoons hot water
1 teaspoon vanilla extract
2 eggs
1 egg white
Vegetable cooking spray

Combine first 8 ingredients in a large bowl.
Combine coffee granules and hot water in a small
bowl. Stir in vanilla, eggs, and egg white; add to
flour mixture, stirring until well blended.

Turn dough out onto a lightly floured surface,
and knead lightly 7 or 8 times. Shape into a 16-
inch-long roll. Place roll on a baking sheet coated
with cooking spray, and flatten to 1-inch thickness.

Bake at 325° for 30 minutes. Transfer roll to a
wire rack, and let cool 10 minutes. Cut roll diagonally into 30 (½-inch) slices; place slices, cut sides
down, on baking sheet. Bake 10 minutes. Turn
cookies, and bake 10 additional minutes (cookies
will be slightly soft in center but will harden as
they cool). Remove cookies from baking sheet, and
let cool completely on wire rack. Yield: 2½ dozen.

PER COOKIE: 75 CALORIES (16% FROM FAT)
FAT 1.3G (SATURATED FAT 0.2G)
PROTEIN 2.0G   CARBOHYDRATE 13.7G
CHOLESTEROL 15MG   SODIUM 67MG

Orange-Pistachio Baklava

ORANGE-PISTACHIO BAKLAVA

This variation of a Middle Eastern classic has half the fat of the original. Cooking spray replaces butter between the layers of phyllo.

Butter-flavored vegetable cooking spray
1¼ cups chopped pistachios
¾ cup wheat saltine cracker crumbs (about 20 crackers)
⅓ cup sugar
½ teaspoon ground cinnamon
12 sheets frozen phyllo pastry, thawed
2 tablespoons margarine, melted
¾ cup honey
½ cup frozen orange juice concentrate, thawed and undiluted
⅓ cup water
1 teaspoon ground cinnamon
⅛ teaspoon ground cloves

Coat a 13- x 9- x 2-inch baking pan with cooking spray; set aside.

Combine pistachios, cracker crumbs, sugar, and cinnamon in a bowl; stir well, and set aside.

Working with 1 phyllo sheet at a time, lightly coat each sheet with cooking spray. Fold phyllo sheet in half crosswise to form a 13- x 8½-inch rectangle; lightly coat both sides of rectangle with cooking spray. Place in bottom of pan; sprinkle 3 tablespoons pistachio mixture over phyllo. Repeat procedure with 9 sheets of phyllo, cooking spray, and remaining pistachio mixture, working with 1 sheet at a time and ending with pistachio mixture.

Lightly coat remaining 2 sheets of phyllo with cooking spray. Fold each sheet in half crosswise to form a 13- x 8½-inch rectangle; lightly coat both sides of each rectangle with cooking spray. Layer each into baking pan.

With a very sharp knife, score diamond shapes, ¾ inch deep, into layers of phyllo. Drizzle margarine over phyllo. Bake at 350° for 25 minutes or until golden.

Combine honey and remaining 4 ingredients in a small saucepan; bring to a boil. Reduce heat; simmer, uncovered, 5 minutes, stirring frequently. Remove from heat; drizzle honey mixture over phyllo. Cool completely in pan. Cut into 16 (3¼- x 2¼-inch) bars. Yield: 16 bars.

PER BAR: 220 CALORIES (35% FROM FAT)
FAT 8.5G (SATURATED FAT 1.2G)
PROTEIN 3.9G   CARBOHYDRATE 33.9G
CHOLESTEROL 0MG   SODIUM 143MG

Perfect Pastries

Phyllo dough can be tricky to handle when preparing baklava, Apple Strudel (page 133), and other pastries. Here's how to use it successfully. First, thaw the dough thoroughly, and then work on a dry surface with one sheet of phyllo at a time. Keep the remaining dough covered with a damp (not wet) cotton towel to prevent it from drying out. Any unused phyllo can be rewrapped and frozen.

ANZAC BISCUITS

1 cup all-purpose flour
½ teaspoon baking soda
1 cup regular oats
1 cup firmly packed brown sugar
½ cup shredded sweetened coconut
¼ cup stick margarine, melted
3 tablespoons water
2 tablespoons golden cane syrup or
    light-colored corn syrup
Vegetable cooking spray

Combine first 5 ingredients in a bowl; stir well. Add margarine, water, and syrup; stir well. Drop by level tablespoonfuls 2 inches apart onto baking sheets coated with cooking spray. Bake at 325° for 12 minutes or until almost set. Let stand 2 to 3 minutes or until firm. Transfer cookies from baking sheets to wire racks, and let cool completely. Yield: 2 dozen.

Note: We found these Australian cookies were much better when made with golden cane syrup. Cane syrup is thicker and sweeter than corn syrup and can be found in supermarkets, in cans, next to the jellies and syrups or in stores specializing in Caribbean and Creole cookery.

PER COOKIE: 98 CALORIES (27% FROM FAT)
FAT 2.9G (SATURATED FAT 1.0G)
PROTEIN 1.2G CARBOHYDRATE 17.3G
CHOLESTEROL 0MG SODIUM 59MG

BANANAS FOSTER

½ cup unsweetened apple juice
⅛ teaspoon apple pie spice
2 medium-size firm, ripe bananas, peeled and
    split lengthwise
1¼ teaspoons cornstarch
1 tablespoon rum
⅛ teaspoon maple flavoring
⅛ teaspoon butter flavoring
2 cups vanilla nonfat frozen yogurt

Combine apple juice and apple pie spice in a large skillet. Add bananas to juice mixture; cook over medium heat 2 minutes or just until bananas are heated, basting frequently with juice.

Combine cornstarch, rum, and flavorings; add to banana mixture. Cook, stirring constantly, 1 minute or until slightly thickened. Scoop ½ cup frozen yogurt into each individual bowl. Top yogurt evenly with banana mixture. Yield: 4 servings.

PER SERVING: 156 CALORIES (2% FROM FAT)
FAT 0.3G (SATURATED FAT 0.1G)
PROTEIN 4.1G CARBOHYDRATE 36.6G
CHOLESTEROL 0MG SODIUM 63MG

LEMON GELATI

Gelati is Italy's version of ice cream.

1 cup sugar
1 tablespoon grated lemon rind
⅛ teaspoon salt
⅔ cup fresh lemon juice
1½ cups plain nonfat yogurt
Fresh mint sprigs (optional)

Combine first 4 ingredients in a bowl; stir until sugar dissolves. Add yogurt; stir well. Pour mixture into freezer container of a 1- or 2-quart hand-turned or electric freezer. Freeze according to manufacturer's instructions. Garnish with mint, if desired. Yield: 5 (½-cup) servings.

Note: Serve gelati in lemon shells, if desired. To prepare shells, trim bottoms of 5 whole lemons so they stand up. Cut off top third of lemons, and scoop out pulp, leaving shells intact. Place lemon shells, upside down, on paper towels until well drained. Spoon frozen gelati into lemon shells, and freeze until firm.

PER SERVING: 201 CALORIES (0% FROM FAT)
FAT 0.1G (SATURATED FAT 0.1G)
PROTEIN 4.0G CARBOHYDRATE 48.2G
CHOLESTEROL 1MG SODIUM 111MG

Lemon Gelati

HONEY-GRAPEFRUIT GRANITÀ

This Italian version of an ice will have a slightly granular texture typical of that dessert.

4 cups fresh pink grapefruit juice (from about
   10 large grapefruit)
1⅓ cups Basic Sugar Syrup
⅓ cup honey

Combine juice and Basic Sugar Syrup in a large bowl; stir well, and set aside.

Place honey in a small bowl. Microwave at HIGH 30 seconds or until warm. Add to juice mixture; stir well. Pour mixture into a 13- x 9- x 2-inch baking dish; cover and freeze at least 8 hours or until firm.

Remove mixture from freezer, and scrape entire mixture with the tines of a fork until fluffy. Spoon into a container; cover and freeze up to 1 month. Yield: 12 (½-cup) servings.

BASIC SUGAR SYRUP
1 cup plus 2 tablespoons sugar
1 cup water

Combine sugar and water in a saucepan; stir well. Bring mixture to a boil; cook, stirring constantly, 1 minute or until sugar dissolves. Yield: 1½ cups.

PER SERVING: 124 CALORIES (1% FROM FAT)
FAT 0.1G (SATURATED FAT 0.0G)
PROTEIN 0.5G   CARBOHYDRATE 31.9G
CHOLESTEROL 0MG   SODIUM 1MG

FYI

The frozen desserts on pages 128 through 131 may be soft after freezing, but ripening will harden the mixture and allow flavors to blend. To ripen a frozen dessert, spoon the frozen mixture into freezer-safe containers. Stir lightly, and then cover and freeze for 1 to 2 hours before eating.

RASPBERRY-CHAMPAGNE SORBET

1 cup water, divided
¾ cup sugar
2 cups fresh raspberries
2 cups champagne, chilled

Combine ¾ cup water and sugar in a small saucepan; bring to a boil, stirring until sugar melts. Remove from heat, and let cool completely.

Position knife blade in food processor bowl; add raspberries and remaining ¼ cup water. Process until smooth. Strain and discard seeds.

Combine sugar mixture, raspberry puree, and champagne. Pour mixture into freezer container of a 2-quart hand-turned or electric freezer. Freeze according to manufacturer's instructions. Let ripen 1 hour. Yield: 8 (½-cup) servings.

PER SERVING: 132 CALORIES (1% FROM FAT)
FAT 0.2G (SATURATED FAT 0.0G)
PROTEIN 0.5G   CARBOHYDRATE 23.0G
CHOLESTEROL 0MG   SODIUM 3MG

PRALINES AND CREAM ICE MILK

¾ cup chopped pecans, divided
½ cup sugar
Vegetable cooking spray
⅔ cup sugar
2 cups 1% low-fat milk
1 cup evaporated skimmed milk
½ cup frozen egg substitute, thawed
1 teaspoon vanilla extract

Place ½ cup pecans in container of an electric blender; cover and process until finely chopped.

Place ½ cup sugar in a small saucepan over medium-high heat. Cook about 3 minutes or until sugar melts and is golden, stirring frequently. Stir in finely chopped pecans. Rapidly spread mixture onto a baking sheet coated with cooking spray. Cool pecan mixture completely.

Pralines and Cream Ice Milk

Break mixture into small pieces. Place in container of an electric blender; cover and process until finely ground.

Spoon into a bowl. Coarsely chop remaining ¼ cup pecans; stir into praline mixture. Set aside.

Combine ⅔ cup sugar and remaining 4 ingredients in a bowl; beat at medium speed of an electric mixer until well blended. Pour milk mixture into freezer container of a 2-quart hand-turned or electric freezer; freeze according to manufacturer's instructions. Spoon into a freezer-safe container; stir in praline mixture. Cover and let ripen at least 2 hours. Yield: 14 (½-cup) servings.

PER SERVING: 141 CALORIES (31% FROM FAT)
FAT 4.8G (SATURATED FAT 0.6G)
PROTEIN 3.9G CARBOHYDRATE 21.6G
CHOLESTEROL 2MG SODIUM 52MG

Apple Strudel

APPLE STRUDEL

½ cup raisins
¼ cup brandy
3 tablespoons hot water
1 teaspoon sugar
1 pound Granny Smith apples, cored, peeled,
   and coarsely chopped
¼ cup firmly packed light brown sugar
¼ cup fine, dry breadcrumbs, toasted
1 teaspoon grated lemon rind
1 teaspoon ground cinnamon
⅓ cup margarine
¼ cup honey
12 sheets frozen phyllo pastry, thawed
Vegetable cooking spray
Lemon balm sprigs (optional)

Combine raisins, brandy, water, and sugar in a small bowl. Let stand 30 minutes or until raisins are plump. Drain; discard liquid. Combine raisin mixture, apple, and next 4 ingredients in a bowl; toss well. Set aside. Combine margarine and honey in a small saucepan. Place over medium heat until margarine melts, stirring occasionally.

Place one sheet of phyllo on wax paper (keeping remaining phyllo covered). Brush phyllo with margarine mixture. Layer 5 sheets of phyllo on first sheet, brushing each sheet with margarine mixture.

Spoon half of apple mixture along edge of one short side of phyllo, leaving a 1-inch border on short side and a 2-inch border on long sides. Fold long sides of phyllo inward.

Starting with short side, roll phyllo, jellyroll fashion. Coat a 15- x 10- x 1-inch jellyroll pan with cooking spray. Transfer strudel to jellyroll pan; brush with margarine mixture. Repeat procedure with remaining phyllo, margarine mixture, and apple mixture to make a second strudel. Bake 30 minutes or until golden. (Shield ends of strudel with aluminum foil, if necessary, to prevent excessive browning.) Cool slightly; garnish with lemon balm, if desired. Cut each strudel into 8 slices to serve. Yield: 16 servings.

PER SERVING: 151 CALORIES (29% FROM FAT)
FAT 4.9G (SATURATED FAT 0.9G)
PROTEIN 1.5G   CARBOHYDRATE 24.3G
CHOLESTEROL 0MG   SODIUM 130MG

APPLE BISCUIT TATIN

¼ cup firmly packed dark brown sugar
2 tablespoons reduced-calorie margarine
6 large Granny Smith apples (about 2½
   pounds), peeled, cored, and cut into eighths
2 tablespoons cornstarch
2 teaspoons ground cinnamon
2 tablespoons brown sugar
1 cup sifted cake flour
¼ cup yellow cornmeal
1 teaspoon baking powder
½ teaspoon baking soda
¼ cup sugar
¼ cup margarine
¼ cup plain nonfat yogurt
¼ cup skim milk

Combine ¼ cup brown sugar and 2 tablespoons reduced-calorie margarine in a 10-inch cast-iron skillet. Cook over medium heat until mixture bubbles, stirring frequently.

Combine apple, cornstarch, and cinnamon in a large bowl; toss gently. Layer apple mixture in skillet; sprinkle with 2 tablespoons brown sugar.

Combine flour and next 4 ingredients in a bowl, stirring well. Cut in ¼ cup margarine with a pastry blender until mixture resembles coarse meal. Combine yogurt and milk; add to flour mixture, stirring with a fork just until dry ingredients are moistened.

Drop dough by spoonfuls over apple mixture. Bake at 375° for 35 to 45 minutes or until apple is tender and crust is golden. (Shield with aluminum foil to prevent excessive browning, if necessary.) Serve warm. Yield: 10 servings.

PER SERVING: 211 CALORIES (28% FROM FAT)
FAT 6.5G (SATURATED FAT 1.2G)
PROTEIN 1.9G   CARBOHYDRATE 38.2G
CHOLESTEROL 0MG   SODIUM 156MG

Pear Galette

PEAR GALETTE

Bring this "free-form" pie to the table before cutting—it crumbles when sliced.

1½ cups all-purpose flour
2 tablespoons granulated sugar, divided
¼ teaspoon salt
¼ cup chilled stick margarine, cut into 4 pieces
3½ to 4 tablespoons ice water
Vegetable cooking spray
⅓ cup firmly packed brown sugar
¼ cup cornstarch
⅛ teaspoon ground cloves
6 medium-size ripe Bosc pears (about 2½ pounds), peeled, cored, and cut into 1-inch wedges

Position knife blade in food processor bowl; add flour, 1 tablespoon granulated sugar, and salt. Pulse 2 to 3 times or until combined. Add margarine; pulse 10 times or until mixture resembles coarse meal. With processor running, slowly add ice water through food chute, processing just until combined. (Do not form a ball.)

Gently press two-thirds of flour mixture into a 4-inch circle on heavy-duty plastic wrap; cover with additional plastic wrap. Repeat procedure with remaining flour mixture.

Roll larger portion of dough, still covered, into an 11-inch circle. Place dough in freezer 5 minutes or until plastic wrap can be easily removed. Remove bottom sheet of plastic wrap. Place dough on a baking sheet coated with cooking spray, and remove top sheet of plastic wrap.

Combine brown sugar, cornstarch, and cloves in a small bowl. Sprinkle dough with one-third of brown sugar mixture. Arrange half of pear wedges over dough, leaving a 2-inch border; sprinkle with one-third of brown sugar mixture. Repeat layering procedure with remaining pear wedges and brown sugar mixture.

Roll remaining dough, still covered, into a 10-inch circle. Place dough in freezer 5 minutes or until plastic wrap can be easily removed. Remove bottom sheet of plastic wrap. Place dough over pear wedges; remove top sheet of plastic wrap. Bring edges of bottom layer of dough over top layer of dough; pinch edges to seal.

Cut 6 slits in top of dough to allow steam to escape. Lightly coat top of dough with cooking spray; sprinkle with remaining 1 tablespoon granulated sugar. Bake at 375° for 45 minutes or until lightly browned. Let cool 20 minutes on a wire rack. To serve, cut into wedges. Yield: 10 servings.

PER SERVING: 212 CALORIES (22% FROM FAT)
FAT 5.2G (SATURATED FAT 0.9G)
PROTEIN 2.2G CARBOHYDRATE 40.7G
CHOLESTEROL 0MG SODIUM 115MG

FYI

The names of the pastries and pies on pages 133 through 135 are as delightful as their flavors. These dessert titles also indicate the country where each originated. Apple Strudel is popular in Germany and Austria, while Apple Biscuit Tatin and Pear Galette are favorites in France. Strawberry-Rhubarb Slump, an old recipe from New England, resembles today's fruit cobbler. Each recipe provides under 225 calories and less than 30 percent fat per serving.

STRAWBERRY-RHUBARB SLUMP

1 cup all-purpose flour
1 teaspoon baking powder
¼ teaspoon baking soda
Dash of salt
¼ cup sugar
¼ cup chilled stick margarine, cut into small pieces
¼ cup plus 2 tablespoons low-fat buttermilk
¼ teaspoon almond extract
3 cups whole strawberries, hulled
3 cups sliced rhubarb
½ cup sugar
½ cup water
1 tablespoon cornstarch
2 tablespoons port or other sweet red wine
1 tablespoon sliced almonds
2 teaspoons sugar

Combine first 5 ingredients in a bowl; cut in margarine with a pastry blender until mixture resembles coarse meal. Add buttermilk and extract, and toss with a fork until dry ingredients are moistened. Set dough aside.

Combine strawberries, rhubarb, ½ cup sugar, and water in a 10-inch ovenproof skillet; cover and cook over medium heat 10 minutes, stirring occasionally. Combine cornstarch and wine, stirring well; add to fruit mixture. Bring to a boil, and cook, stirring constantly, 1 minute or until thickened.

Drop dough by heaping tablespoonfuls onto fruit mixture; cover and cook over low heat 10 minutes. Remove from heat, and sprinkle sliced almonds and 2 teaspoons sugar over dumplings and fruit mixture. Broil 5½ inches from heat (with electric oven door partially opened) 3 minutes or until golden. Yield: 8 servings.

Note: If fresh rhubarb isn't available, frozen is a suitable substitute. Apple juice or cider may be used instead of port or sweet red wine.

PER SERVING: 225 CALORIES (26% FROM FAT)
FAT 6.7G (SATURATED FAT 1.2G)
PROTEIN 3.0G CARBOHYDRATE 39.6G
CHOLESTEROL 0MG SODIUM 119MG

RAVIOLI DOLCI

The dough for this sweet ravioli is more like pastry than pasta. This recipe hails from the eastern heel region of Italy.

2½ cups raisins
¼ cup sweet Marsala wine
¼ cup honey
3 tablespoons chopped almonds
2 tablespoons semisweet chocolate
    mini-morsels
½ teaspoon grated lemon rind
4 cups all-purpose flour
¼ teaspoon salt
½ cup sugar
½ cup chilled stick margarine, cut into small
    pieces
2 eggs, lightly beaten
½ cup plus 3 tablespoons ice water, divided
1 egg
1 tablespoon water
Vegetable cooking spray
1 tablespoon powdered sugar

Combine first 6 ingredients; stir well. Let stand 1 hour, stirring occasionally.

Position knife blade in food processor bowl; add raisin mixture. Process until smooth; set aside.

Combine flour, salt, and sugar in a large bowl, and cut in chilled margarine with a pastry blender. Combine 2 eggs and ¼ cup ice water, and add to flour mixture, stirring well. Sprinkle remaining ¼ cup plus 3 tablespoons ice water, 1 tablespoon at a time, over surface of flour mixture; toss with a fork until a dough forms. Gently press dough into a ball. Turn dough out onto a lightly floured surface, and knead lightly 4 or 5 times. Wrap in heavy-duty plastic wrap, and chill 30 minutes.

Combine 1 egg and 1 tablespoon water. Beat with a wire whisk, and set aside. Divide dough into 20 equal portions. Working with 1 portion of dough at a time, roll each into a 4-inch circle on a lightly floured surface.

Spoon 1 rounded tablespoon raisin mixture onto half of each circle; moisten edges of dough with water. Fold dough over filling; press edges together with a fork dipped in flour to seal. Carefully place on baking sheets coated with cooking spray. Brush tops with egg mixture. Bake at 350° for 30 minutes or until lightly browned. Cool on wire racks; sprinkle with powdered sugar. Yield: 20 servings.

PER SERVING: 250 CALORIES (24% FROM FAT)
FAT 6.7G (SATURATED FAT 1.5G)
PROTEIN 4.6G CARBOHYDRATE 44.0G
CHOLESTEROL 33MG SODIUM 96MG

KEY LIME PIE

You can use the slightly yellowish Key limes from the Florida Keys or regular limes to make this pie.

Graham Cracker Crust
1 teaspoon unflavored gelatin
2 tablespoons cold water
½ cup fresh lime juice
2 egg yolks
1 (14-ounce) can fat-free sweetened condensed
    milk
3 egg whites
¼ teaspoon cream of tartar
⅛ teaspoon salt
⅓ cup sugar
Lime slices (optional)

Prepare Graham Cracker Crust; set aside.

Sprinkle gelatin over cold water in a small bowl; set aside. Combine lime juice and egg yolks in a small heavy saucepan. Cook over medium-low heat, stirring constantly, 10 minutes or until slightly thick and very hot (180°); do not boil. Add softened gelatin to lime juice mixture; cook 1 minute, stirring until gelatin dissolves. Place pan in a large ice-filled bowl; stir gelatin mixture 3 minutes or until mixture reaches room temperature (do not allow gelatin mixture to set). Strain gelatin mixture into a medium bowl; discard any solids. Gradually add milk, stirring with a whisk until blended (mixture will be very thick); spoon mixture into Graham Cracker Crust, and spread evenly.

Beat egg whites, cream of tartar, and salt at high speed of an electric mixer until foamy. Gradually add sugar, 1 tablespoon at a time, beating until stiff peaks form. Spread over filling, sealing to edge of

Key Lime Pie

crust. Bake at 325° for 25 minutes; let cool 1 hour on a wire rack. Chill 3 hours or until set. Cut with a sharp knife dipped in hot water. Garnish with lime slices, if desired. Yield: 8 servings.

GRAHAM CRACKER CRUST

2 tablespoons sugar
1 tablespoon chilled stick margarine
1 egg white
1¼ cups graham cracker crumbs
1 teaspoon ground cinnamon
Vegetable cooking spray

Combine first 3 ingredients in a medium bowl; beat at medium speed of an electric mixer until blended. Add crumbs and cinnamon; toss with a fork until moistened. Press crumb mixture into a 9-inch pieplate coated with cooking spray. Bake at 325° for 20 minutes or until lightly browned; let cool on a wire rack. Yield: 1 (9-inch) crust.

PER SERVING: 290 CALORIES (14% FROM FAT)
FAT 4.4G (SATURATED FAT 1.1G)
PROTEIN 7.5G   CARBOHYDRATE 65.1G
CHOLESTEROL 61MG   SODIUM 230MG

STRAWBERRIES AND CREAM CRÊPES

3 cups sliced fresh strawberries
⅓ cup granulated sugar
⅔ cup light process cream cheese, softened
⅓ cup plus 1 tablespoon sifted powdered
   sugar, divided
¾ cup nonfat sour cream
½ teaspoon grated lemon rind
1 tablespoon fresh lemon juice
6 Dessert Crêpes

Combine strawberries and granulated sugar in a bowl; stir well. Cover and chill 1 hour.

Combine cream cheese and ⅓ cup powdered sugar in a bowl; beat at medium speed of an electric mixer until blended. Add sour cream, lemon rind, and lemon juice; beat until smooth. Spread ¼ cup cream cheese mixture over half of each crêpe, and top with ½ cup strawberry mixture. Fold crêpe in half over strawberry mixture. Sprinkle crêpes with remaining 1 tablespoon powdered sugar. Serve immediately. Yield: 6 servings.

DESSERT CRÊPES

1¼ cups all-purpose flour
1 tablespoon sugar
1½ cups skim milk
1 tablespoon margarine, melted
1 egg
Vegetable cooking spray

Combine flour and sugar in a medium bowl; stir well. Combine milk, margarine, and egg, stirring well; add milk mixture to flour mixture, stirring with a wire whisk until almost smooth. Cover batter, and chill 1 hour or overnight.

Coat an 8-inch crêpe pan or nonstick skillet with cooking spray, and place over medium-high heat until hot. Remove pan from heat, and pour a scant ¼ cup batter into pan; quickly tilt pan in all directions so batter covers pan with a thin film. Cook about 1 minute.

Carefully lift edge of crêpe with spatula to test for doneness. The crêpe is ready to turn when it can be shaken loose from pan and the underside is lightly browned. Turn crêpe, and cook 30 additional seconds.

Place crêpe on a towel to cool. Repeat procedure with remaining batter.

Stack crêpes between single layers of wax paper or paper towels to prevent sticking. Cooled crêpes can be stacked in wax paper and frozen in a zip-top plastic bag for up to three months. Yield: 12 crêpes.

PER SERVING: 248 CALORIES (22% FROM FAT)
FAT 6.1G (SATURATED FAT 2.9G)
PROTEIN 8.0G   CARBOHYDRATE 40.4G
CHOLESTEROL 34MG   SODIUM 195MG

For crêpes, add milk, margarine, and egg to flour mixture; stir until smooth. Chill 1 hour.

Pour about ¼ cup batter into a preheated pan, tilting pan so batter covers the bottom.

Lift edge of crêpe to check for doneness—the underside should be light brown. Turn and cook 30 seconds.

TIRAMISÙ
(pictured on page 2)

A combination of low-fat dairy products substitutes for mascarpone, a triple-cream cheese that is traditionally used in this dessert.

½ cup sugar
1 cup nonfat cottage cheese
1 cup nonfat sour cream
1 (8-ounce) carton vanilla low-fat yogurt
1 (8-ounce) package Neufchâtel cheese
2 tablespoons dark rum
1¼ cups hot water
1 tablespoon plus ½ teaspoon instant espresso coffee granules
40 ladyfingers
½ teaspoon unsweetened cocoa

Position knife blade in food processor bowl; add first 6 ingredients. Process until smooth; set aside.

Combine hot water and espresso granules in a small bowl. Split ladyfingers in half lengthwise. Quickly dip 20 ladyfinger halves, cut side down, into espresso; place, dipped side down, in bottom of a 9-inch square baking dish. Dip 20 more ladyfinger halves, cut side down, into espresso; arrange dipped side down, on top of first layer. Spread 2 cups cheese mixture evenly over ladyfingers; repeat procedure with remaining ladyfinger halves, espresso, and cheese mixture.

Place a wooden pick in each corner and one in center of Tiramisù (to prevent plastic wrap from sticking to cheese mixture); cover with plastic wrap. Chill 3 to 8 hours. Remove wooden picks; sprinkle with cocoa. Cut into squares to serve. Yield: 9 servings.

PER SERVING: 222 CALORIES (30% FROM FAT)
FAT 7.5G (SATURATED FAT 4.3G)
PROTEIN 9.9G CARBOHYDRATE 25.8G
CHOLESTEROL 79MG SODIUM 254MG

FLAN
(pictured on page 122)

Flan is a traditional dessert served in the Spanish-speaking countries.

1⅓ cups sugar, divided
¾ cup frozen egg substitute, thawed
¾ teaspoon vanilla extract
2 (12-ounce) cans evaporated skimmed milk
Vanilla bean (optional)

Place 1 cup sugar in a large heavy skillet over medium heat; cook 5 minutes or until sugar dissolves (do not stir). Continue cooking until golden, and stir well. Immediately pour into a 9-inch round cakepan, tilting quickly until sugar coats bottom of cakepan; set aside.

Combine remaining ⅓ cup sugar, egg substitute, vanilla extract, and milk; stir well. Pour into prepared cakepan; place cakepan in a large, shallow pan. Add hot water to pan to depth of 1 inch. Bake at 350° for 1 hour or until a knife inserted near center comes out clean. Remove cakepan from water; let cool 1 hour on a wire rack. Cover and chill 4 hours.

To serve, loosen edges of flan with a knife. Place a serving plate, upside down, on top of cakepan; invert flan onto plate. Drizzle any remaining syrup over flan. Garnish with vanilla bean, if desired. Cut into wedges to serve. Yield: 8 servings.

PER SERVING: 207 CALORIES (1% FROM FAT)
FAT 0.2G (SATURATED FAT 0.1G)
PROTEIN 8.7G CARBOHYDRATE 43.3G
CHOLESTEROL 3MG SODIUM 132MG

Cut the Fat

An easy way to lower fat in desserts is to use reduced-fat products in place of regular high-fat versions. Our favorites include nonfat sour cream, nonfat and low-fat yogurt, Neufchâtel cheese, and evaporated skimmed milk.

Bread Pudding with Whiskey Sauce

BREAD PUDDING WITH WHISKEY SAUCE

3½ cups skim milk
¾ cup sugar
¾ cup frozen egg substitute, thawed
½ cup raisins
2 tablespoons vanilla extract
1 teaspoon ground cinnamon
1 teaspoon butter flavoring
9 (1-ounce) slices French bread, cut into
  ¾-inch cubes
2 tablespoons margarine, melted
Vegetable cooking spray
Whiskey Sauce

Combine first 7 ingredients in a large bowl; stir. Add bread cubes, and toss gently. Let stand 1 hour.

Add margarine; toss gently. Spoon mixture into a 13- x 9- x 2-inch baking dish coated with cooking spray. Bake at 350° for 45 minutes or until pudding is set. Serve warm or at room temperature. Cut into 12 squares, and place on individual dessert plates; top with Whiskey Sauce. Yield: 12 servings.

WHISKEY SAUCE

¼ cup sugar
½ cup unsweetened apple juice
¼ cup bourbon
2 tablespoons margarine
⅛ teaspoon ground cinnamon
⅔ cup water
2½ teaspoons cornstarch

Combine sugar and next 4 ingredients in a small saucepan. Cook over medium heat, stirring frequently, until sugar dissolves. Combine water and cornstarch; stir well, and add to apple juice mixture. Bring to a boil, and cook, stirring constantly, 1 minute. Serve warm. Yield: 1½ cups.

Note: Substitute 1 tablespoon rum extract and 3 tablespoons water for bourbon, if desired.

PER SERVING: 226 CALORIES (18% FROM FAT)
FAT 4.4G (SATURATED FAT 1.0G)
PROTEIN 6.1G CARBOHYDRATE 39.3G
CHOLESTEROL 2MG SODIUM 229MG

INDEX

METRIC EQUIVALENTS

Metric Equivalents for Different Types of Ingredients

A standard cup measure of a dry or solid ingredient will vary in weight depending on the type of ingredient. A standard cup of liquid is the same volume for any type of liquid. Use the following chart when converting standard cup measures to grams (weight) or milliliters (volume).

Standard Cup	Fine Powder (ex. flour)	Grain (ex. rice)	Granular (ex. sugar)	Liquid Solids (ex. butter)	Liquid (ex. milk)
1	140 g	150 g	190 g	200 g	240 ml
¾	105 g	113 g	143 g	150 g	180 ml
⅔	93 g	100 g	125 g	133 g	160 ml
½	70 g	75 g	95 g	100 g	120 ml
⅓	47 g	50 g	63 g	67 g	80 ml
¼	35 g	38 g	48 g	50 g	60 ml
⅛	18 g	19 g	24 g	25 g	30 ml

Useful Equivalents for Liquid Ingredients by Volume

¼ tsp							=	1 ml	
½ tsp							=	2 ml	
1 tsp							=	5 ml	
3 tsp	=	1 tbls			=	½ fl oz	=	15 ml	
		2 tbls	=	⅛ cup	=	1 fl oz	=	30 ml	
		4 tbls	=	¼ cup	=	2 fl oz	=	60 ml	
		5⅓ tbls	=	⅓ cup	=	3 fl oz	=	80 ml	
		8 tbls	=	½ cup	=	4 fl oz	=	120 ml	
		10⅔ tbls	=	⅔ cup	=	5 fl oz	=	160 ml	
		12 tbls	=	¾ cup	=	6 fl oz	=	180 ml	
		16 tbls	=	1 cup	=	8 fl oz	=	240 ml	
	1 pt	=	2 cups	=		16 fl oz	=	480 ml	
	1 qt	=	4 cups	=		32 fl oz	=	960 ml	
						33 fl oz	=	1000 ml	= 1 l

Useful Equivalents for Dry Ingredients by Weight

(To convert ounces to grams, multiply the number of ounces by 30.)

1 oz	=	¹⁄₁₆ lb	=	30 g
4 oz	=	¼ lb	=	120 g
8 oz	=	½ lb	=	240 g
12 oz	=	¾ lb	=	360 g
16 oz	=	1 lb	=	480 g

Useful Equivalents for Cooking/Oven Temperatures

	Fahrenheit	Celcius	Gas Mark
Freeze Water	32° F	0° C	
Room Temperature	68° F	20° C	
Boil Water	212° F	100° C	
Bake	325° F	160° C	3
	350° F	180° C	4
	375° F	190° C	5
	400° F	200° C	6
	425° F	220° C	7
	450° F	230° C	8
Broil			Grill

Useful Equivalents for Length

(To convert inches to centimeters, multiply the number of inches by 2.5.)

1 in				=	2.5 cm	
6 in	=	½ ft		=	15 cm	
12 in	=	1 ft		=	30 cm	
36 in	=	3 ft	= 1 yd	=	90 cm	
40 in				=	100 cm	= 1 m